A Barna Report
Produced in Partnership w

Children's Ministry In A New Reality

Building Church Communities That Cultivate Lasting Faith

Funding for this research was made possible by the generous support of Awana. Barna Group was solely responsible for data collection, analysis and writing of the report.

Table of Contents

Preface by Awana

In your life and ministry, do you know your core question?

As in, something that captivates your curiosity or pulls at your heart to become the leader, minister, craftsman or artist you are? Maybe it is a question you think about on a regular basis and are cognizant of nearly each day. Or perhaps you are a driven leader who has yet to pause long enough to dig under your get-it-done drive and ask yourself what that question really is.

But your question is there—and it's a core part of your life pursuit as one created in God's image.

My wife and I have a core question, and it's one we've been trying to answer since the late 1990s: *What does the local church do in children's ministry that is most likely to form lasting faith in children?*

Throughout the last couple of decades, we've taken on a variety of roles within children's ministry: small group leader, large group teacher, Sunday school teacher, greeter, Awana volunteer, elementary ministry director, preschool volunteer, parents'-day-out team member, VBS volunteer, church consultant, church trainer, parenting ministry volunteer, conference director, children's ministry curriculum publisher and child discipleship nonprofit executive. As we've journeyed together for over two decades, the roles within children's ministry have changed, but our pursuit of the answer to this question has grown with curiosity and increased focus.

Three Key Factors That Form Resilient Faith in Children

Ultimately, our journey led us to join the leadership team at Awana. Our team has been pursuing the answer to the question above with laser-like focus since 2013. This research partnership with Barna Group is an extension of that effort to learn what the local church can do to have an enduring impact on kids' faith—to understand *Children's Ministry in a New Reality*.

In Awana's prior research, we found three primary factors that, when simultaneously present, give children a greater likelihood of forming lasting faith in Jesus Christ. We speak of these three primary child discipleship factors as *Belong, Believe, Become.*

- *Belong*—relationships, community and Kingdom
- *Believe*—scripture engagement that leads to trusting faith in Jesus Christ
- *Become*—experiences to live in God's presence and live out faith

Said another way: Child discipleship is designed to form lasting faith by helping kids *belong* to God and his Kingdom, *believe* in Jesus Christ as Lord and savior and to *become* like Jesus and walk in his ways.

The goal of next-generation ministries (from birth to young adulthood) in the local church is to form lasting faith, and that's precisely what's happening when kids interact with loving, caring adult disciplemakers and find a path to belong, believe and become. We continue to see, including in these pages, that when a church cultivates a highly relational intergenerational community that cares deeply for children, engages the scripture together and offers real-life experiences, children have an opportunity to be formed as followers of Jesus.

Rapid Identity Formation in a Post-Christian Culture

In an episode of our *Resilient Disciples* podcast, Barna CEO David Kinnaman remarked, "The Church is woefully unprepared for Gen Z."

I believe David is completely accurate in his assessment. Why? While local church leaders long to form children (now the leading edge of "Generation Alpha") into apprentices of Jesus, the reality is that the dominant secular culture is a powerful force, competing to form children into hyper-individualists. Especially in our post-iPhone world, the mobile device has become like an interstate system through which secularism cruises—and, friends, it's rush hour.

Simply stated, the challenge for the Church is that our current children's ministry systems were designed for a different era. Most of our children's ministry systems were designed in what you might call a majority-Christian culture with a heavy "programmatic" blueprint that lends itself to what's called "edutainment." Gen Z and now Gen Alpha need a different system, one that's blueprinted for highly relational engagement.

As it's been said, disciples make disciples.

Shifting Our Thinking to New Realities

As I read the data from the following research, like you, I'm not only thinking of today; I'm thinking of the Church of 2050. If today's kids are to be the church members and even the Church leaders of 2050, how should we change our thinking?

Instead of thinking of what the church does as "children's ministry" (or "KidMin"), what if we shifted our thinking to "child discipleship?" Child discipleship is specific, timeless and lasting. It's a well defined target and mission. In our post-Christian culture, there's a need for greater specificity and intentionality.

I believe this study contains some significant findings as it pertains to the fruitfulness of our discipleship of children and our need to reimagine and reinforce children's ministry. Our prayer for you as you engage this data is that you will be captivated by new insights that help you and your team build a child discipleship ministry that forms lasting faith. Thank you for your work. We believe the kids you are discipling today will engage the culture and lead the fearless future of the Church. I can't think of any ministry more formative than that.

Matt Markins
Awana, President & CEO

Introduction by Barna Group

What is the "new reality" the title of this book refers to?

According to Barna Group's research, it's a reality in which people are both more online and lonelier. It's a time when more Americans, especially young adults, are eschewing religion but embracing spiritual curiosity. Of course, at this moment, it's a world that is reeling from a pandemic and figuring out new ways of navigating community.

All of the above trends have profound impact in the U.S. Church and, by extension, children's ministries in the U.S.

The new reality means the youngest of churchgoers can swipe to open a device before they can write their name. In the past couple years, many in the emerging generation have reached milestones in their childhood or their education in untraditional ways—from a distance, from behind a mask or from a computer at home. These children are coming of age in a secularizing society, and they may encounter big intellectual questions about culture and faith at earlier ages and with more possible sources for answers.

The new reality means kids are being raised by Millennial and Gen X parents who may have waited longer than previous adult generations to start families. They come to child-rearing with a rich, unique set of experiences in life and career, a mistrust of institutions and perhaps even their own turbulent journey with doubts about Christianity or the Church.

The new reality means that, as these caregivers contemplate their role in the faith formation of their household and their children, they look for help from a Church that is waning and evolving. Church dropouts have been on the rise long before the pandemic pushed congregations headlong into online and hybrid ministry options. Pastors and church leaders cling to their callings in an era where their credibility is in question, their audience is distracted and their job description is increasingly complicated.

This is the climate in which today's Christians are tasked to transfer lasting, resilient faith. And it *is* possible.

It will require unprecedented imagination and collaboration in approaches to children's ministry, but Barna's research and this book—produced in partnership with Awana—offer fresh, encouraging findings for sharing and shaping faith among children.

In Barna's previous research focused on understanding the next generation, we've surveyed parents, pastors and teenagers. For *Children's Ministry in a New Reality*, we chose to add an important and more specific survey audience. We conducted a comprehensive study among just children's ministry leaders (that is, Protestant church leaders who indicate having decision-making responsibility for their church's children's ministry).

We didn't want to gather more hunches about how kids' ministry is conducted. So, we went to the source, to the men and women trusted by churches to help facilitate the spiritual formation of kids today. How are they doing? In what areas are they confident, and in what areas are they confused or ill-equipped? What is the reality of their work, and do they feel they are making an impact?

Transferring a lasting, resilient faith will require unprecedented imagination and collaboration in approaches to children's ministry

In addition to this tighter research focus on children's ministry leaders, we also zoomed out, strategically broadening the scope of our survey of congregants beyond just those with a child in a kids' ministry program and inviting the whole Church into this study. We asked churched adults in general (those who have attended a service in the past six months) to weigh in on the state of child discipleship today.

In early discussions with our partners at Awana, we wondered if children's ministry is being integrated into the rest of the church or if it is regarded as, well, child's play. Do congregants have conviction and awareness about the opportunities to disciple children? Is there a perceived hierarchy that implies the discipleship of older generations is somehow more serious or more important? Are there certain groups within the church whose participation or interest in child discipleship is assumed (or not)? We knew we needed to talk to a wide swath of churchgoers—old and young, men and women, married and single, with and without children in the home, committed and occasional attendees—to answer these questions and to contextualize kids' ministry within the U.S. Church, on a national and local level.

Of course, parents and guardians are essential partners in developing young disciples. So, we oversampled within our survey of churched adults to listen closely to those who indicate having a children's-ministry-aged child in the home (specifically, ages 5–14-years-old). These parents, guardians and caregivers give us of-the-moment insight into the actual influence of children's ministry. They help us gauge expectations vs. reality, and they allow for a full-circle view of faith formation—from the church, to the home and back again.

Through the responses of these groups and in the following pages, you'll see the urgent need for a new, shared vision for child discipleship. Along the way, children's ministry experts and practitioners expand on the findings and offer practical examples and recommendations.

Within local churches today, there are startling gaps in the responsibility and resources for child discipleship—and yet, already within the pews, there are also remarkable provisions to fill those gaps and build the future Church. ●

At a Glance

Children's ministry leaders know their work is of great importance

64% strongly agree churches cannot grow without effective children's ministry.

. . . and parents and guardians feel the same.

More than half (54%) say their child's time in ministry is just as important as their own experience in service.

But measures for success are hazy

Most children's ministry leaders say it's either somewhat difficult (48%) or only somewhat easy (40%) to evaluate the impact on children.

. . . and the responsibilities of child discipleship are disputed.

More than nine in 10 children's ministry leaders say the home is the source of discipleship, while parents look equally to both the church and the home.

Kids' ministries need more focus and support

56% of children's ministry leaders agree at least somewhat that children's ministry is often forgotten by their church.

. . . and their leaders may need to be reminded of their influence and impact.

Just 15 percent of children's ministry leaders—compared to 36 percent of parents of 5–14-year-olds—consider themselves "very influential" in a child's development.

The whole Church is on board with the primary objective of children's ministry

There is consensus that, above all else, children should leave a kids' program "knowing that Jesus loves them."

. . . and their willingness to build strong, intergenerational relationships may be a key to resilient discipleship.

Two-fifths of children in children's ministry have a meaningful relationship with an adult—which correlates with deeper engagement with the Church, with the Bible and with community. ●

CHAPTER 1

CHILDREN'S MINISTRY MATTERS—BUT WHY?

The stakes have never been higher, and the standards for success have never been blurrier

Walk into any church in the U.S., and you will most likely find an option for children's ministry. Overall, 80 percent of churches have a children's ministry, and 81 percent have a youth ministry, according to congregants. Other programs for groups like married adults, college students or seniors, though still available in many churches, are far less common than ministry for kids and youth.

Children's ministry's ubiquitous presence is tied to its unmistakable priority. It is seen as one of the most important things, if not *the* most important thing, in a church. Ask anyone—ministry leaders, congregants, parents and guardians.

Barna Group did, and we found widespread agreement.

Nearly two-thirds of children's ministry leaders (64%) go so far as to strongly agree churches cannot grow without an effective children's ministry. Even in decisions about facilities, church plants or building expansions, children's ministry spaces are by far the top consideration.

Children's ministry leaders:
"Churches cannot grow without effective children's ministry."

● Agree strongly   ● Agree somewhat

64%	25%

n=600 U.S. children's ministry leaders, June 8–August 16, 2021.

Likewise, the majority among churched parents of 5–14-year-olds says the children's ministry was "very" important in their selection of their church (62%). Assuming their church can only focus on a couple of programs, a similar majority (61%) says children's ministry would be most important (comparatively, youth ministry is selected by 48% and adult ministry by 38%). Though this percentage declines somewhat when the sample includes non-parents (who are, naturally, more interested in adult ministry), children's ministry is still chosen by half of all congregants (51%) as the most important focus of a church, making this the top response overall in a list of age-specific or affinity church programs.

That's not to say parents don't have priorities in the broader context of a church, including their own experience. Rather, the majority (54%) strongly agrees a kid's time in children's ministry is just as important as a parent's time in the sanctuary.

Why, exactly, do they see the weekly hour or so that kids spend in a specialized service—singing, learning, playing—as so pivotal?

Parents of 5–14-year-olds: When selecting the church you currently attend, how important was children's ministry in the selection process?

● Very important ● Somewhat important ● Somewhat unimportant
● Not at all important ● Not sure

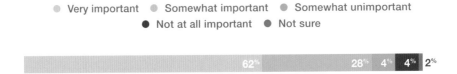

62%   28%   4%   4%   2%

n=1,021 U.S. churched adults with a child ages 5–14 at home, June 11–July 6, 2021.

Parents of 5–14-year-olds: "Their time in children's ministry is as important as my time in service."

● Agree strongly ● Agree somewhat

54%   34%

n=1,021 U.S. churched adults with a child ages 5–14 at home, June 11–July 6, 2021.

There Is a Looming Discipleship Deadline

Throughout the Church, there is a great sense of urgency (and, at times, worry) about discipleship in the childhood years . There is good reason for this.

First: Childhood and teen years are primary seasons for faith formation. Looking back on their own spiritual journeys, respondents consistently select the 7–17 age range as peak years when they were discipled, an experience that is far less common once adulthood arrives. Adults who are now children's ministry leaders are especially likely to recall seasons of discipleship in the early years of life; 53 percent say they were discipled between ages 7 and 12, and 67 percent say they were discipled between ages 13 and 17.

> Children's ministry is seen as one of the most important things, if not *the* most important thing, in a church

Research supports these recollections and underscores the sensitivity and importance of forming faith in early years. Past research conducted by George Barna, in fact, concluded that spiritual beliefs are largely set by the time someone reaches 13 years of age.[1] It's not a new idea that childhood, pre-teen and early teen years are crucial for development—but there are new cultural forces and shifts that add complexity to this truth.

Across the course of your life, have you been discipled at any of the following age ranges?

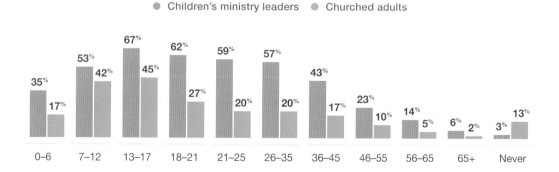

● Children's ministry leaders   ● Churched adults

Age range	Children's ministry leaders	Churched adults
0–6	35%	17%
7–12	53%	42%
13–17	67%	45%
18–21	62%	27%
21–25	59%	20%
26–35	57%	20%
36–45	43%	17%
46–55	23%	10%
56–65	14%	5%
65+	6%	2%
Never	3%	13%

n=600 U.S. children's ministry leaders, June 8–August 16, 2021;
n=2,051 U.S. churched adults, June 11–July 6, 2021.

Second: Leaders and churchgoers are reckoning with unprecedented challenges facing kids today—for example, the prevalence and impact of digital devices among a generation of "digital natives." Parents believe it's never been harder to raise kids, and their number one reason is technology and social media.[2] At least 40 percent of respondents regard social media (47% children's ministry leaders, 40% churched adults) and the internet (44%, 41%) as "very" influential in a child's development. Put in context, congregants place church on par (at best) with digital forces in terms of influence on kids, while children's ministry leaders assume their own influence is paltry by comparison (see page 58 for more).

Third: Children's ministries are both affected by—and able to affect—an exodus from the Church. Barna has committed much study to "church dropouts," those who grew up in church but then withdrew from church involvement in adulthood, even if just for a time. That group has grown, alongside broader secularization in the U.S. Among young adults (ages 18–29), the dropout rate sits at an alarming 64 percent.[3] That's nearly two-thirds among a cross-section of Millennials and Gen Z who had a Christian background and then, at least for a season, bowed out of the Church. In their absence, percentages of atheists, agnostics and "nones" are on the rise, especially among the leading edge of Gen Z.

Research led by Barna president David Kinnaman reveals that just 10 percent of 18–29-year-olds with a Christian background qualify as "resilient disciples," a category of committed, faithful, engaged young Christians who keep showing up. This exemplary minority is exactly that: the minority. We learn much from what they have in common, however: The young adults who stay share the increasingly rare but important experience of finding belonging in a church and grasping the relevance of their faith early in life.

It makes sense, then, that children's ministry leaders worry about a potential exodus of young churchgoers and their crucial role in helping churches avoid it. Two-fifths (39%) strongly agree, and a further half (49%) somewhat agrees, that they are concerned children will leave the faith as adults.

All things considered, you can't blame children's ministry leaders and parents for feeling they are up against a key deadline in discipleship. They have a keen sense that children's ministry impacts the heart of both the present and future Church in the U.S.

Children's ministry leaders: "I am concerned that children will leave their Christian faith when they become adults."

● Agree strongly   ● Agree somewhat

39%   49%

n=600 U.S. children's ministry leaders, June 8–August 16, 2021.

Yet, as Barna's research suggests and as we'll explore throughout this report, children's ministry is also a precarious and misunderstood element of ministry and church life, with a tremendous need for support and clarity.

Children's ministry leaders worry about a potential exodus of young churchgoers

Let's begin with one of the most confused aspects of children's ministry: how to assess its effectiveness.

Leading Ministry with a Moving Target

Encouragingly, children's ministry leaders have a hunch that their work is indeed making a long-term difference in kid's lives (45% "definitely," 42% "somewhat"). Churched adults, especially parents of 5–14-year-olds, agree in even higher numbers.

Leaders could use a boost, however, in precisely evaluating their impact. Few (8%) say it's very easy to do so. Instead, most say it's either somewhat difficult (48%) or only somewhat easy (40%) to evaluate impact.

"I am hopeful that we are grounding kids in the love of God and understanding that they are loved, and that they are able to share love in the world. I think that makes a difference in their lives—but I find it hard to measure," one children's ministry leader stated.

Open-ended responses allowed children's ministry leaders to share some of the ways they discern their impact and effectiveness. Across all responses, parental involvement / family engagement is mentioned most often as a critical determinant of outcomes. Many of the leaders' suggested indicators of impact

The Long-Term Impact of Children's Ministry

● Yes, definitely   ● Yes, somewhat   ● Maybe   ● No

Children's ministry leaders: Do you feel like your ministry is making a long-term difference in children's lives?
45% 42% 11% 2%

All churched adults: Do you feel like the children's ministry at your church is making a long-term difference in children's lives?
59% 29% 10% 2%

Parents of 5–14-year-olds: Do you feel like the children's ministry at your church is making a long-term difference in children's lives?
64% 26% 8% 2%

n=600 U.S. children's ministry leaders, June 8–August 16, 2021; *n*=2,051 U.S. churched adults, June 11–July 6, 2021.

Children's ministry leaders: How easy or difficult is it to evaluate the impact children's ministry is having on children?

● Very easy   ● Somewhat easy   ● Somewhat difficult   ● Very difficult

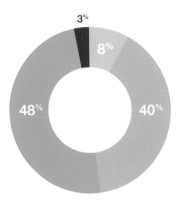

n=600 U.S. children's ministry leaders, June 8–August 16, 2021.

are subjective or difficult to get a handle on, such as "excitement." Several leaders mention having faith that their work must have long-term impact because they believe the Word of God does not return void (Isaiah 55:11).

"Some of it is intangible," one leader acknowledged, "but when we hear kids delight in Bible lessons, that reminds us that we are on the right track."

Still, many children's ministry leaders say it's difficult to lead knowing they may never see the fruits of their work or that children may drop out of their program regardless of their efforts.

It's interesting to note that children's ministry leaders' sense of satisfaction and support hangs together with the ability to assess their impact. The majority of those who are completely satisfied in vocational ministry (77%) or the level of support they receive from church leadership (62%) and the congregation (64%) find it very or somewhat easy to evaluate the impact they're having. Those with low levels of satisfaction (69% with ministry, 72% with support from church leadership, 62% with support from congregation) usually find it somewhat or very difficult to evaluate impact. This study can't define the direction of that relationship—if satisfaction and support stem from having strong metrics for impact, or if strong metrics for impact stem from having satisfaction and support. But we do see that clear measures for evaluating effectiveness in children's ministry are a quality of supportive, satisfying church environments.

Jesus First ... Right?

There are at least some clues as to what both children's ministry leaders and churched adults, including parents, believe matters most in a children's ministry.

Let's begin with the end in mind: If a child fully engages in a church, what should they have gained by the time they "age out" of children's ministry?

The goal, leaders and churched adults strongly agree, is to know that Jesus loves them. Similarly, having a personal relationship with Jesus and an understanding of their redemption through him surface high on the list of possible gifts a child should take with them after kids' ministry.

> Clear measures for evaluating effectiveness in children's ministry are a quality of supportive, satisfying church environments

Another desired goal is simply for children to be equipped to "graduate" into the continuing experience of the church. A successful engagement with children's ministry, leaders and churched adults feel, should leave someone feeling like a part of the church body or feeling comfortable joining either a main worship service or youth ministry.

Other possible outcomes—having a loving, caring relationship with an adult, understanding the Bible, engaging culture—appear lower on the list. (As we'll learn on page 70, however, healthy, meaningful relationships between kids and mentoring adults are not to be neglected and could be key in setting kids up for resilient faith.)

For the most part, children's ministry leaders and churched adults alike resonate with these "takeaways" of children's ministry in a similar order, though children's ministry leaders are more emphatic across the board that these are things their programs should provide.

Imagine a child who actively engages with everything a ministry offers. When they age out of children's ministry, they should . . .

% strongly agree

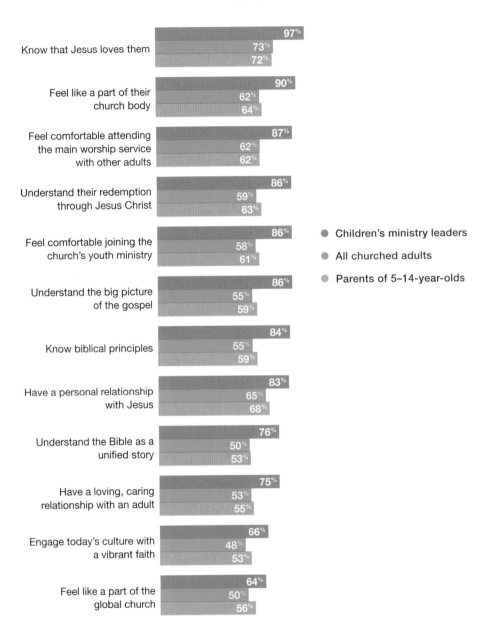

Know that Jesus loves them
97%
73%
72%

Feel like a part of their church body
90%
62%
64%

Feel comfortable attending the main worship service with other adults
87%
62%
62%

Understand their redemption through Jesus Christ
86%
59%
63%

Feel comfortable joining the church's youth ministry
86%
58%
61%

● Children's ministry leaders

● All churched adults

● Parents of 5–14-year-olds

Understand the big picture of the gospel
86%
55%
59%

Know biblical principles
84%
55%
59%

Have a personal relationship with Jesus
83%
65%
68%

Understand the Bible as a unified story
76%
50%
53%

Have a loving, caring relationship with an adult
75%
53%
55%

Engage today's culture with a vibrant faith
66%
48%
53%

Feel like a part of the global church
64%
50%
56%

n=600 U.S. children's ministry leaders, June 8–August 16, 2021;
n=2,051 U.S. churched adults, June 11–July 6, 2021;
n=1,021 U.S. churched adults with a child ages 5–14 at home, June 11–July 6, 2021.

From other angles, we continue to see that nurturing a relationship with Jesus is considered the main aim of children's ministry. Asked to select the most important aspects of children's ministry, children's ministry leaders' top choice is "children making a personal relationship with Jesus" (47% rank this first). Similarly, the next most-selected aspect is "children's salvation," though this is chosen by a much lower percentage (18%).

When asked what the parents and guardians in their church see as most important, however, children's ministry leaders believe that children's safety is paramount to parents (26%), above a personal relationship to Jesus (18%) or kids' salvation (15%).

That's not actually the case, parents and guardians themselves say. In their own ranking of the most important aspects of children's ministry, their top goal is aligned with children's ministry leaders': helping children develop a personal relationship with Jesus (24%). Nine percent, meanwhile, place child safety at the top of the list.

Something has been lost in translation here. Children's ministry leaders have received the message that, above all, parents and guardians care that their children are in a safe environment. This isn't a wildly off-base assumption; physical and spiritual safety in kids' programs is essential, and parents indeed stress safety, in many forms, as a priority. For instance, in Barna's 2016 *The State of Youth Ministry* report, parents' foremost hope for youth groups was that their kids would find "safe spaces" to explore faith and have positive relationships.

Here, however, parents and children's ministry leaders tell us they share a primary objective: to help children know and grow with Jesus.

Nurturing a relationship with Jesus is considered the main aim of children's ministry

We're left with a compelling if hazy picture of what the Church today expects of children's ministry. On the one hand, there is consensus that children's ministry is crucial—in the life of the child and the health of a church—and that it should nurture a relationship with Jesus. On the other hand, there is a profound need for closer alignment, collective participation and clearer evaluation when it comes to moving toward this worthy goal. ●

REFLECTIONS

Process these questions on your own, with your team or with stakeholders in your children's ministry

- Given that children's ministry corresponds with a short but formative time in the life and discipleship of an individual, what should be the most important aspects of your ministry? How should they look, sound and feel? Would that be different from your current approach?

- What do you see as potential threats to the faith of the children in your church and community? What steps can you and your team take to help mitigate these potential threats?

- How would you describe "success" as a children's ministry leader or volunteer? Are you experiencing this? How would you measure this goal?

- Do you feel your children's ministry is making an impact weekly? For the long term? After kids age out of children's ministry? Why or why not?

- Many parents feel their time in service and their child's time in children's ministry are equally important. What are the differences or similarities across the experiences of adults or children in your church? Do you feel the services have similar levels of commitment, attention, support or impact?

SPECIAL SECTION: An Invitation to Children's Ministry Services

Join us to learn what children's ministries are like at present—the lessons, practices and experiences that are foundations for kids' faith formation today

"When?"
Every Weekend (Maybe)
Three in five churched parents of 5–14-year-olds (58%) say their child attends a service, activity or program through their church at least once a week; 17 percent are engaging multiple times a week. Another 27 percent report that their child shows up monthly, or multiple times a month.

"Where?"
Usually in Person, Sometimes Online
As of summer 2021, when this survey was conducted, the majority of children's ministry leaders (78%) indicated their program was completely in-person while one in five (20%) continued in a hybrid approach. Some children's ministries, such as those in urban environments, have been slower to resume gathering since the onset of COVID-19, with 15 percent operating entirely online. Still, knowing the majority of children's ministries has at least some in-person element, we can assume the survey provides a good picture of the standard children's ministry gathering at present.

Usually, parents say, children are participating in a church service (55%), and vacation Bible school (45%) and children's choir (31%) are other popular options. Roughly one-fifth sends their child to a mid-week program (24%) or some other type of program (19%).

"What?"
Faith, Fun & Food for Thought
According to children's ministry leaders, some of the core activities in services revolve around introducing kids to the Bible: studying it, reading it aloud, discussing texts. Other group activi-

ties—praying together, singing together, playing games, having fun—are also regular occurrences. Deeper scriptural engagement, such as committing Bible verses to memory or learning about a biblical worldview, are less common. Crafts are less frequently part of services, though 43 percent of children's ministries still offer this activity weekly.

Children's ministry leaders: In your children's ministry, how often do you do any of the following?

● Weekly   ● A few times a week   ● Monthly   ● Once every few months
● Less often   ● Never

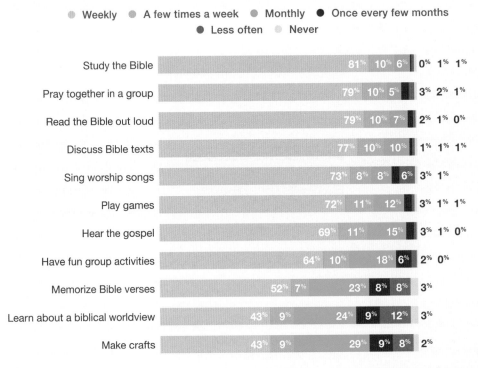

	Weekly	A few times a week	Monthly	Once every few months	Less often	Never
Study the Bible	81%	10%	6%	0%	1%	1%
Pray together in a group	79%	10%	5%	3%	2%	1%
Read the Bible out loud	79%	10%	7%	2%	1%	0%
Discuss Bible texts	77%	10%	10%	1%	1%	1%
Sing worship songs	73%	8%	8%	6%	3%	1%
Play games	72%	11%	12%	3%	1%	1%
Hear the gospel	69%	11%	15%	3%	1%	0%
Have fun group activities	64%	10%	18%	6%	2%	0%
Memorize Bible verses	52%	7%	23%	8%	8%	3%
Learn about a biblical worldview	43%	9%	24%	9%	12%	3%
Make crafts	43%	9%	29%	9%	8%	2%

n=600 U.S. children's ministry leaders, June 8–August 16, 2021.

Parents of 5–14-year-olds, perhaps because of a limited or secondhand view of what may be occurring in children's ministries, provide a somewhat different assessment than leaders when selecting what their kids participate in at church. Specifically, they assume there is less engagement with scripture than is reported by children's ministry leaders. They are also less likely than children's ministry leaders to report their child's participation in any church activity on a *weekly* basis.

In terms of sacraments or milestones in their child's faith, the majority of parents of 5–14-year-olds says their child has personally accepted Jesus as their savior (80%), been baptized (68%) or been confirmed (63%).

Parents of 5–14-year-olds:
How often does your child do each of the following?

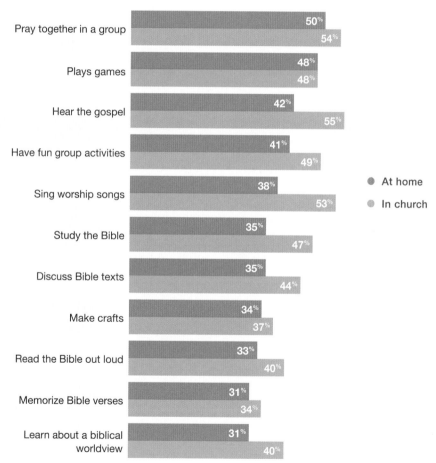

% say their child does this activity weekly

Activity	At home	In church
Pray together in a group	50%	54%
Plays games	48%	48%
Hear the gospel	42%	55%
Have fun group activities	41%	49%
Sing worship songs	38%	53%
Study the Bible	35%	47%
Discuss Bible texts	35%	44%
Make crafts	34%	37%
Read the Bible out loud	33%	40%
Memorize Bible verses	31%	34%
Learn about a biblical worldview	31%	40%

● At home
● In church

n=1,021 U.S. churched adults with a child ages 5–14 at home, June 11–July 6, 2021.

Encouragingly, it seems some of the practices in a child's Sunday service are also regular activities in their daily routine at home. Beyond recreation such as games or fun in groups, half of parents of 5–14-year-olds report that their child is engaging in group prayer at home (50%). Though church is consistently a more likely environment for biblical study and spiritual activity, about two in five kids hear the gospel (42%) and sing worship songs (38%) in their home during a given week,

Families are also taking home conversations and materials related to what kids learn in children's ministry. Whether because a parent initiates the conversation (42% every time, 34% most times) or because a child shares unprompted (31% every time, 43% most times), a child's attendance at a church class or program usually results in more discussion when they go home. Many weeks, there will also be some kind of material provided to parents to help facilitate these conversations and support their child's spiritual development. Two in five parents of 5–14-year-olds say this occurs every week (39%), and another two in five say this happens monthly (38%). ◉

Q&A: THE GOALS & VALUES OF CHILDREN'S MINISTRY

Q: Why does children's ministry matter in the big picture of the Church and especially in this moment?

A: The reason why I would say children's ministry matters is because we live in a culture where family is in great peril. Even when kids aren't being abandoned physically, they're being abandoned in many ways, including emotionally and spiritually.

I think kid's ministry plays a part in finding kids who have been abandoned and pulling them into a family, which is the Church, and helping them experience what a healthy family looks like. Kids' ministry, through the act, art and vehicle of discipleship, should help grow and develop kids—and in turn, parents and families—to reflect the Church, which is a family.

Often in the New Testament, when Paul talks about the Church, he does it in terms of a family. The Church is an actual family. God is the Father. Christ is our brother. It's all family language, even in the Trinity.

Q: Many church leaders say that churches cannot grow without an effective children's ministry, and nearly nine in 10 parents of 5–14-year-olds agree "My children's time in children's ministry is just as important as my time in service." Does this ring true to you? Do you see church staff and parents behaving in a way that matches the significance they place on children's ministry?

SAM LUCE

Sam has been involved in children's ministry and youth ministry since 1997. Currently, he serves as the global pastor of ministries at Redeemer Church. In addition to discipling families, he helps equip kids' pastors and family ministry through his blog at SamLuce. com. Sam is a frequent speaker at conferences, has published numerous articles, and co-authored several books. He is passionate about the clarity of the gospel, the importance of the Church and being the best dad and husband for his family.

A: I think this rings true in the way children's ministry currently is. However, I'm not sure if that's the way it should be. I think there is some unhealthiness there.

Children's ministry, in meeting a legitimate need in some senses, has also created an unintended sense of unhealthiness because parents have come to abdicate their discipleship responsibilities to the church. And some children's pastors agree with this, saying, "I'm the person who understands kids and knows how to work with kids. Give your kids to me, and I'll give them back to you as a Christian." I don't know if those are good consequences.

I believe these consequences are a byproduct of a Church that has lost its ability to disciple adults who then disciple their children. I think the reason people think we need kids' ministry is because we don't have well-discipled adults who are discipling others. If we had adults who were discipling their children, kids' ministry would be *helpful, but not necessary*. But because we don't have discipled adults who are in turn discipling their kids, kids' ministry is necessary.

> "We have created a faith that is simplified. It's a faith that kids grow out of instead of a robust faith that they grow into."

As much as I am an advocate for kids' ministry, I have no problem with not having kids' ministry in a church that is aware that children are our responsibility and led by a pastor who is aware that there are children in the room.

Another problem I've witnessed with the specialization of children's ministry is that we have created a faith that is simplified. It's a faith that kids grow out of instead of a robust faith that they grow into. Because of the desire to make things understandable, relatable and relevant to kids, we have removed mystery. We've removed paradox. When they bump up against something difficult, the simple Jesus they learned about when they were five can no longer help them in the complex world of their 20s, and so we inoculate them from the gospel.

I think that we give kids a cheap substitute by simplifying Jesus down to this 2-D object that we can manage, and it's really idolatry in some ways because Jesus becomes a god that we can control and manage.

Q: Half of children's ministry leaders say it is at least somewhat difficult for them to evaluate the impact children's ministry is having on children. This points to a need for clear or new metrics. Why is it so difficult to measure progress or success in children's ministry? What are some ways that children's ministry leaders can effectively measure the impact children's ministry is having on kids' lives?

A: As a quick response, I would share that the Church in America has often reduced the metric of success to how many people come.

Another metric kids' pastors use is to gauge how many children had fun. We tailor our service around wanting to see more children come, and in order to do that, we want them to have more fun so they invite their friends.

The metrics children's ministry leaders should use should align closer to these questions: Do students know the Ten Commandments? Do they know the Apostles' Creed? Do they know the Lord's Prayer? These are three core tenets of every catechism.

The reason why we don't have any metrics other than attendance is that most churches have expunged catechism from their church. It's seen as a dead form, but it's a tangible way to measure that kids have internalized the Christian faith. Whether kids fully understand isn't as important as the fact that they've internalized a theologically accurate grid by which they can see the world and God's work.

When our church starts catechism in preschool and goes through college with it, I want students to memorize that first question of the Heidelberg. I want them to memorize the Ten Commandments. I want them to memorize the Apostles' Creed. Because these are the things by which they're going to be able to recognize heresy and things that aren't true in the world.

The new metrics we need are not just turnout numbers, but how we have faithfully handed children the faith given to us. How well have children received the faith and applied it to their lives?

Q: Parents, guardians and children's ministry leaders are aligned in saying that the number one thing a kid should leave children's ministry with is the knowledge that Jesus loves them. What do you see as other goals of children's ministry? What should they have or know when they age out?

A: I would say they need to understand the historic faith handed to them. I think the knowledge that Jesus loves them is not what kids need to know when they get out of kids' ministry. That's what they need to know when they get out of preschool.

What kids need to know when they get out of kids' ministry is the biblical, theological arc of scripture. They need to know that God created a perfect world. We broke it. Jesus redeems it, and one day he'll come back to glorify it. They need to understand by the time they leave that Jesus is going to make all things new, he is at work in our life now doing that, and he will ultimately renew all things. They need to know the historic faith handed to us through the different creeds because those are foundational for us to understand scripture.

They need to understand the faith handed to them, but they also need to have an experience with Jesus that is personal, living and active, so they know he is not just an object to be studied, but a person to be known. ●

CHAPTER 2

STOPPING THE STALEMATE

Children's ministry leaders and parents don't always agree on the domain of faith formation

Who exactly bears the most responsibility for the task of child discipleship—in either its success or failure?

To children's ministry leaders, the answer seems plain. A dominant 95 percent of these leaders say the home should be the primary environment for discipleship. Thus, when children do leave their Christian faith, children's ministry leaders often assume parents and guardians came up short in some way. Parents did not model discipleship to kids, half of children's ministry leaders (49%) assume, making this their top explanation for church dropouts. Or perhaps parents weren't engaged enough in the church, one in three children's ministry leaders says (35%). About one-quarter acknowledges various negative associations with church itself—disenchantment, discipleship gaps or a lack of relationships—may prompt kids to leave faith. Even then, children's ministry leaders examine the church's possible influence only after suggesting children themselves simply never took responsibility for their faith.

> 95 percent of children's ministry leaders say the home is the primary source of discipleship. Churched adults, especially parents, aren't so sure.

On the other hand, churched adults aren't so sure the household is the beating heart of discipleship. Just over half (55%) agree discipleship should

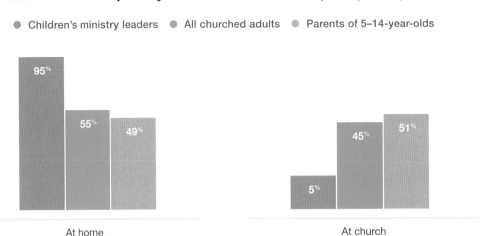

Where should the primary source of children's discipleship take place?

● Children's ministry leaders   ● All churched adults   ● Parents of 5–14-year-olds

95%
55%
49%

At home

5%
45%
51%

At church

n=600 U.S. children's ministry leaders, June 8–August 16, 2021;
n=2,051 U.S. churched adults, June 11–July 6, 2021;
n=1,021 U.S. churched adults with a child ages 5–14 at home, June 11–July 6, 2021.

primarily occur at home, while another 45 percent believe it should occur at church (8% are not sure). Parents of 5–14-year-olds—kids in the prime years for children's ministry—are even more split on this point, divvying up responsibility evenly between church (51%) and home (49%). They perhaps recognize their limits as a spiritual leader, with most parents (86%) agreeing, half (47%) strongly so, that their child learns things at church that they cannot teach them.

Churched adults likewise distribute the responsibility for dropouts across a spectrum of options, selecting causes related to the child, their church or their guardians in relatively similar numbers. The plurality responses among churched adults well captures the divide: They assume kids who leave the faith "never felt a sense of belonging in the church" or had parents who "were not engaged enough in the church."

Neither children's ministry leaders nor the parents or guardians of children want to see even more kids walk away from the Church. They hope to see them age out of children's ministry and opt into the broader life of the Church and the blessings of a relationship with Jesus. But parents and

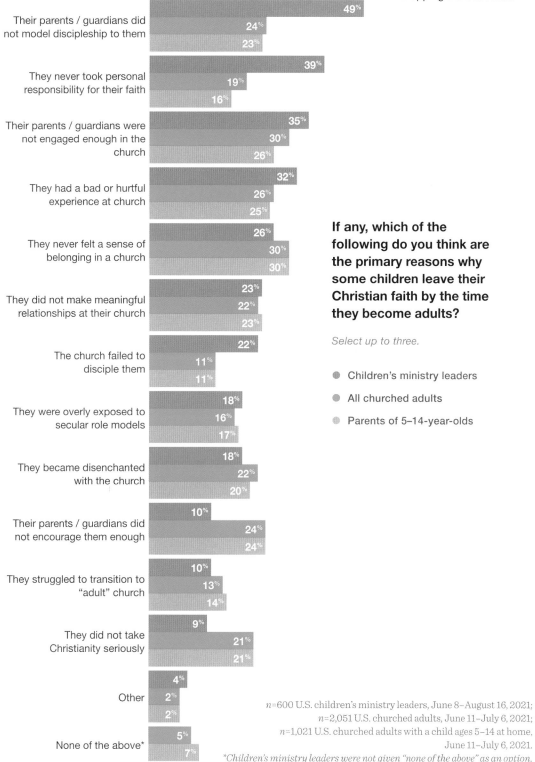

Their parents / guardians did not model discipleship to them
49%
24%
23%

They never took personal responsibility for their faith
39%
19%
16%

Their parents / guardians were not engaged enough in the church
35%
30%
26%

They had a bad or hurtful experience at church
32%
26%
25%

They never felt a sense of belonging in a church
26%
30%
30%

They did not make meaningful relationships at their church
23%
22%
23%

The church failed to disciple them
22%
11%
11%

They were overly exposed to secular role models
18%
16%
17%

They became disenchanted with the church
18%
22%
20%

Their parents / guardians did not encourage them enough
10%
24%
24%

They struggled to transition to "adult" church
10%
13%
14%

They did not take Christianity seriously
9%
21%
21%

Other
4%
2%
2%

None of the above*
5%
7%

If any, which of the following do you think are the primary reasons why some children leave their Christian faith by the time they become adults?

Select up to three.

● Children's ministry leaders

● All churched adults

● Parents of 5–14-year-olds

n=600 U.S. children's ministry leaders, June 8–August 16, 2021;
n=2,051 U.S. churched adults, June 11–July 6, 2021;
n=1,021 U.S. churched adults with a child ages 5–14 at home,
June 11–July 6, 2021.
Children's ministry leaders were not given "none of the above" as an option.

ministry leaders are uncertain at best and opposed at worst when it comes to determining how to partner together and support children in their faith formation.

What will it look like to break this stalemate?

Thinking about who needs to step up in child discipleship, children's ministry leaders and parents seem to point at each other. They might also want to point *outward*. Barna's research suggests that other adults, mentors and friends can be powerful allies in growing kids' faith, creating a "third space" for discipleship between home and church. (In chapter four, we'll bring in some reinforcements.)

Let's Talk About What to Talk About with Kids

The *substance* of child discipleship and the conversations that should accompany faith formation are other areas in which children's ministry leaders and parents aren't entirely aligned.

Barna asked children's ministry leaders about a variety of faith-related topics that might emerge in the teaching or discipleship of the children's program. Specifically, we wondered about the comfort level of both leaders and their helpers in tackling these spiritual conversations at the appropriate time.

For the most part, if it's related to Christianity, the Bible and following Jesus, children's ministry leaders assume both they and their ministry's helpers are on firm footing. In the following chart, you can see this illustrated

MEASURING DISCIPLESHIP

Whoever takes the helm in discipling members of the next generation, there is another important question to answer: How do we effectively measure discipleship, defined for this survey as "the process of modeling and guiding others toward loving and following Jesus?"

Children's ministry leaders' most-selected options, equally, are to monitor children's understanding of the big picture of the gospel in the Bible, their integration of biblical principles into their lives and their awareness of God actively working in their lives. These behavioral responses are more popular than concrete measures, like church attendance or the number of baptisms and confirmations, or interactive measures like engagement with scripture or with other people.

Barna and Awana have partnered on an assessment to help churches and children's ministries better strategize and gauge effectiveness in their approaches to child discipleship. Learn more by scanning the QR code. ●

Please note that this assessment is hosted by our technology partners at Gloo. A free account will be required.

Children's ministry leaders: Please indicate how effective each is in measuring discipleship among children.

% say "very effective"

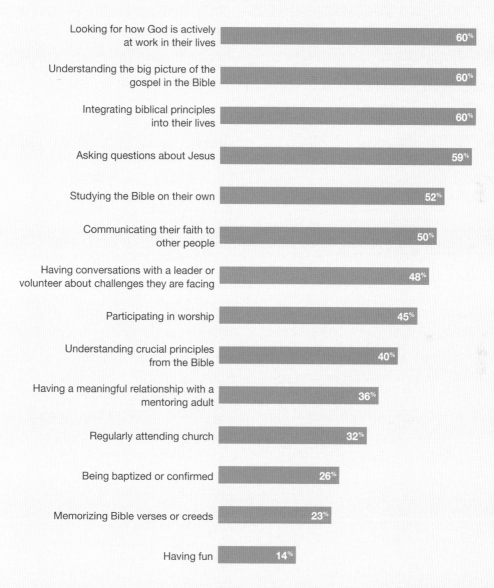

Looking for how God is actively at work in their lives — 60%

Understanding the big picture of the gospel in the Bible — 60%

Integrating biblical principles into their lives — 60%

Asking questions about Jesus — 59%

Studying the Bible on their own — 52%

Communicating their faith to other people — 50%

Having conversations with a leader or volunteer about challenges they are facing — 48%

Participating in worship — 45%

Understanding crucial principles from the Bible — 40%

Having a meaningful relationship with a mentoring adult — 36%

Regularly attending church — 32%

Being baptized or confirmed — 26%

Memorizing Bible verses or creeds — 23%

Having fun — 14%

n=600 U.S. children's ministry leaders, June 8–August 16, 2021.

through two complementary data points: the consistently high percentage of children's ministry leaders who feel *"very"* comfortable covering these items, and the consistently low percentage who say their helpers feel *uncomfortable* covering these items. **The gap between? You could think of it as a safe zone; high confidence, low discomfort. Someone leading or serving on a Sunday morning likely feels they have it under control.**

Children's Ministry Leaders' & Helpers' Comfort Level with Spiritual Topics

● I'm "very" comfortable leading children at the appropriate age in conversations about …

● Children's ministry helpers feel uncomfortable with leading children at the appropriate age in conversations about …

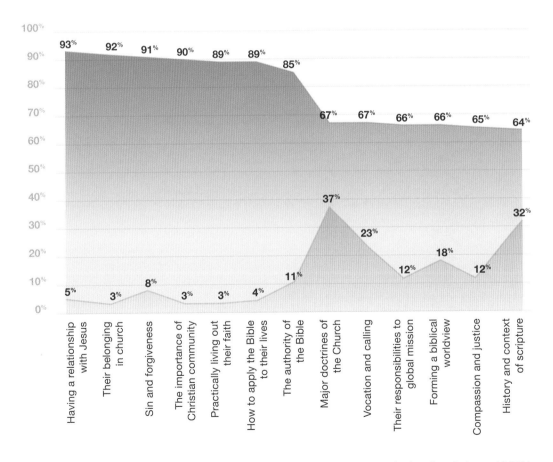

n=600 U.S. children's ministry leaders, June 8–August 16, 2021.

There are a handful of spiritual issues, however, where children's ministry leaders and their helpers are less sure of themselves. For example, we see a pinch in comfort levels surrounding major doctrines of the Church and the history and context of scripture. It's possible these areas fall outside of the training of many children's ministry leaders and volunteers. Perhaps these more formal topics produce concern about getting things wrong. The research shows the majority of children's ministry leaders believes these subjects should be taught in later years—in junior high school at the earliest.

Children's Ministry Leaders' & Helpers' Comfort Level with Social Topics

● I'm "very" comfortable leading children at the appropriate age in conversations about …

◑ Children's ministry helpers feel uncomfortable with leading children at the appropriate age in conversations about …

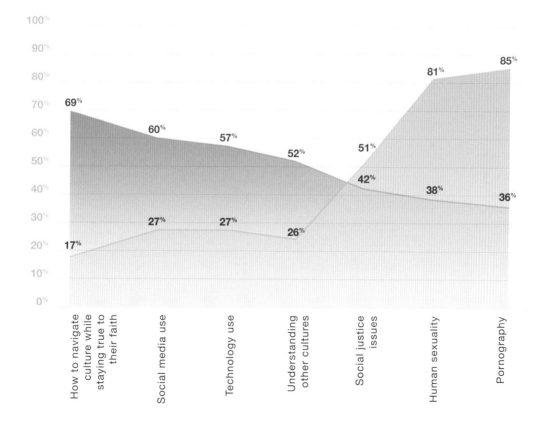

n=600 U.S. children's ministry leaders, June 8–August 16, 2021.

In addition to the spiritual topics covered above, Barna looked at reported comfort levels addressing some *social* issues a children's ministry may be expected to engage with.

As you can see in the chart, discomfort competes with and even exceeds confidence on social issues. Though the majority of children's ministry leaders feels good about helping kids navigate culture while staying true to their faith, they are less certain when presented with specific cultural conversations that may arise. The topics of pornography and sexuality, for instance, fall most outside the comfort zone, and on social justice, the confidence of children's ministry leaders is middling. Again, this could be credited to the fact that children's ministry leaders worry about the appropriate context for these subjects, which most believe begins in junior high school or later.

Clearly, children's ministries today navigate a minefield of potential topics to cover in their lessons and conversations. No wonder 37 percent of leaders agree at least somewhat they are afraid of getting children's discipleship wrong.

Children's ministry leaders:
"I am afraid of getting children's discipleship wrong."

● Agree strongly ● Agree somewhat

n=600 U.S. children's ministry leaders, June 8–August 16, 2021.

In research for the report *Faith Leadership in a Divided Culture*, Barna learned that ministers increasingly report feeling pressure, both internally and externally, to speak out on public or social issues, sometimes before they feel ready to do so.[4] This pressure is no doubt acutely felt by those leaders trying to disciple young digital natives, many of whom are exposed to troubling or at least confusing subjects through the internet more frequently and at earlier ages than ever before.

Each topic carries with it its own set of questions for children's ministry leaders: *What does the Bible have to say about this subject, if anything? Is this something parents and guardians will be OK with me mentioning? What is the right age and right context to tackle this with a student? Am I knowledgeable or confident enough to lead this discussion or answer questions? Is this something to be handled as a whole class, in small groups or individually? What sources, verses or other voices do I need to bring into this conversation? What happens if I say nothing at all?*

As a starting point, we do see that children's ministry leaders and churched adults, including parents of children's-ministry-aged kids, are aligned on whether children's ministries should address difficult topics. Across the board, about three-quarters in each group believes current events, mental health, social issues and other touchy subjects should be open for discussion in church programs for kids.

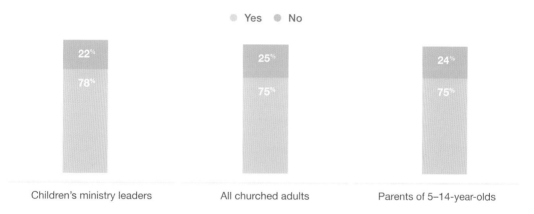

Do you believe children's ministry should address current events, social topics, mental health or potentially difficult subjects?

Yes   No

Children's ministry leaders	All churched adults	Parents of 5–14-year-olds
22% / 78%	25% / 75%	24% / 75%

n=600 U.S. children's ministry leaders, June 8–August 16, 2021; n=2,051 U.S. churched adults, June 11–July 6, 2021; n=1,021 U.S. churched adults with a child ages 5–14 at home, June 11–July 6, 2021.

Barna took inventory of how some of these more difficult topics make their way into children's ministry, comparing the responses of churched parents who hope certain subjects are addressed with those of children's ministry leaders who say they are doing exactly that.

Bullying, loneliness and social media—magnified in an online era—are the most prevalent tough topics in children's ministries. This likely reassures parents, the majority of whom also identifies these as items to be addressed.

On the other end of the spectrum, leaders and parents find another point of agreement: Politics doesn't need to come up in children's ministry.

On nearly every other item, however, parents' beliefs that subjects should be addressed outpaces the children's ministry leaders reports of actually addressing them. The divide is most pronounced on the grave topics of suicide and self-harm.

Are Children's Ministries Covering the Tough Topics That Matter to Parents?

● Children's ministry leaders: % say their children's ministry has addressed this
● Parents of 5–14-year-olds: % believe children's ministry should address this

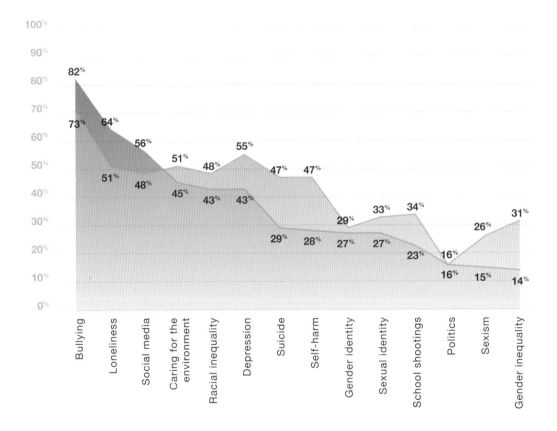

n=600 U.S. children's ministry leaders, June 8–August 16, 2021;
n=1,021 U.S. churched adults with a child ages 5–14 at home, June 11–July 6, 2021.

Parents welcome the Church's partnership in walking with their kids as they face some of the toughest topics

These gaps don't necessarily need to be filled with the input of children's ministers and volunteers alone—additional training, special guests, prayer, counsel, trusted mentors or outside referrals could bolster the Church's credibility and responsibility in these areas. Additionally, just because parents believe a children's ministry should tackle a subject doesn't mean it's the best route for the church, the program or the individual. Ultimately, these data serve as a spotlight on topics that parents recognize as serious, and suggest another area where parents welcome the Church's partnership in walking with their kids as they face some of the toughest topics.

For that partnership to be fruitful, and for churches to help shoulder disciplemaking for the next generation, children's ministries may need some added support themselves. In the following chapter, we'll gain some new perspective on the logistical hang-ups that plague children's ministry leaders. ●

REFLECTIONS

Process these questions on your own, with your team or with stakeholders in your children's ministry

- What are some ways those in the home and church can partner together to help ensure effective child discipleship practices? How can your ministry initiate or be more intentional about these steps?

- Are there any breakdowns in communication or conversation between your children's ministry leaders and volunteers and the parents or guardians of kids? In what areas could you initiate or improve communication?

- How is your ministry equipped to disciple kids on principles of the Christian faith, including basics of doctrine (the truth of the Bible, salvation through Jesus, the role of the Church, etc.)?

- What resources, inside and outside the church, could strengthen the quality, creativity and theology of child discipleship in your congregation?

- How is your children's ministry—and the households it serves—teaching kids to live out their faith? What opportunities are there to model these behaviors in the congregation and in community, and to invite kids as witnesses or participants of faith in action? ●

Q&A: PARTNERSHIPS BETWEEN CHURCHES & HOUSEHOLDS IN DISCIPLESHIP

Q: While 95 percent of children's ministry leaders say the primary source of a child's spiritual development should take place at home, only half of parents with children 4–15-years-old say the same. Why aren't parents and leaders on the same page in terms of where a child's primary spiritual discipleship happens? Do you think they can get there?

A: I fear that leaders in the church have inadvertently sent parents the message that the church is the primary keeper of the spiritual formation of children. We [send this message] with our well-trained leaders, amazing environments, powerful curriculum and life-changing (sometimes flashy) events. The message that many parents receive is, "This is what it takes to foster spiritual formation in children." Sadly, parents, grandparents, guardians and "faith friends" feel like they cannot compete with that or replicate what happens at church. So they step back and defer to the church as the primary provider of spiritual formation of children.

Children's ministry leaders need to not only *tell* parents that they are the primary conduit of spiritual formation. They should also provide resources, opportunities, encouragement and cele-

DR. DENISE MUIR KJESBO

Denise serves as professor and program director at Bethel Seminary in the Master of Arts in Children's and Family Ministry and as the director of The Cory Center for Children's Ministry. Denise is passionate about equipping leaders for their vital calling to serve children and families in church and community.

brations of parents, grandparents, guardians and faith friends as partners in the spiritual formation of children. It may be overwhelming to lay "you are the primary faith nurturers" on parents. Maybe a better approach is to focus on the partnership that we can enjoy together.

Q: Many parents of 5–14-year-olds tell Barna that they recognize their limits as a spiritual leader, with most parents agreeing that their child learns things at church they cannot teach them. How can children's ministry leaders and parents better partner in the discipleship of children? What are some practical ways they can resource each other and work together?

A: I believe churches and parents need to understand each other's "sweet spot" in the spiritual formation of children and celebrate what each other can do.

Families are naturally poised to offer **informal discipleship** in everyday life. They are strategically primed to live out Deuteronomy 6:7. This "teachable moments methodology" of spiritual formation is the most powerful and long lasting. It is the approach that those who live with children can implement best. Healthy relationships in the home provide the foundation for this type of discipleship.

Churches are the natural place for more **formal discipleship**—discipleship that has a plan, curriculum, spaces dedicated to children's ministry as well as gifted, trained and committed leaders. Children's ministry needs to provide what they do best when the children are with them and equip parents to allow the overflow of their life with Jesus to "splash" faith on their children daily in the home.

> "Families are naturally poised to offer informal discipleship in everyday life. Churches are the natural place for more formal discipleship."

The church needs to encourage parents to make discipleship a priority in their own faith journey because parents cannot splash faith out of an empty bucket! Parents, grandparents, guardians and faith friends need to be filled up so that when their children bump into them in daily life, they spill out faith, love for Jesus and the fruit of the Spirit. Then the church needs to provide the connection points for adults in the lives of children through curriculum choices that continue throughout the week, regular prompts with integrated faith formation and tools that are accessible and success-oriented for guardians to use in their homes. The church needs to provide a community for parents to join that encourages them on their path of discipleship and parenting.

Q: When kids walk away from the Church as they grow up, children's ministry leaders tend to assume that parents did not model discipleship to kids; this is their top explanation for church dropouts. Churched adults distribute the blame for the dropout problem across a spectrum of options, selecting causes related to the child, their church or their guardians in relatively similar numbers. Why do you feel there may be this finger-pointing around the issue? How would you suggest leaders and / or households break the stalemate or step up in their own arenas? What do you see as causes of the dropout problem, and how can church and home partner to address it?

A: I think the primary reason for the dropout of youth is the lack of an integrated faith. This means the Church needs to make sure that what is taught on the weekends has feet during the week and connects with the everyday life of the child or youth. Parents need to make sure they don't leave faith formation at the doors of the church when they walk out on a weekend. Parents need to integrate faith into everyday life at home.

Another key component is serving others, because this allows families to put feet to the gospel. The externally focused church movement spoke of this as "People of Good Will, providing Good Deeds, to build a bridge across which the Good News can travel." Service sinks faith deep into the roots of children, youth and adults in families and helps anchor the young person when the time comes for them to make their own decisions about their journey with Jesus.

The Church needs to reevaluate how we display ourselves to children and youth. We also need to remember that this is a marathon, not a sprint. Reconnecting with churched young people around their 30s may be a more accurate picture of seeing them owning their faith for the long haul.

Q: Parents and guardians want churches to dive into tough topics with kids, while the leaders don't always feel ready or equipped. The biggest gap occurs around matters of mental health, depression or anxiety and school shootings;

children's ministries aren't covering these as much as parents would hope. What are a few questions or tips you would encourage a children's ministry leader to filter through to decide if, when or how to tackle tough topics? And why do you feel parents and guardians are looking to the church for help on these subjects?

A: Churches need to listen to the concerns of parents, grandparents, and guardians and provide resources to help them in their journey with children. Helpful podcasts, training opportunities for parents, support and counseling resources for those struggling with mental health issues, and regular listening sessions where church leaders can find out what parents need are great places to start. ●

CHAPTER 3

OVERCOMING OVERWHELM

From volunteer turnout to potential burnout, children's ministry leaders have many (and oft-forgotten) needs

There are strong scriptural reasons that, as the last chapter explored, nearly all children's ministry leaders believe households are the home of child discipleship. "Commit yourselves wholeheartedly to these commands that I am giving you today," Deuteronomy 6:6–9 reads. "Repeat them again and again to your children. Talk about them when you are at home and when you are on the road, when you are going to bed and when you are getting up. Tie them to your hands and wear them on your forehead as reminders. Write them on the doorposts of your house and on your gates."

Still, this study suggests children's ministry leaders could have practical incentive, too, to lean on families and households. Taking on more of a supporting role in child discipleship may appeal to an overwhelming majority of children's ministry leaders when many of them are, indeed, overwhelmed.

Let's zoom out a bit: In January 2021, Barna found that 29 percent of Protestant senior pastors in the U.S. were seriously considering quitting full-time ministry.[5] It seemed a sign of the weight that clergy must shoulder today, especially through a season marked by a pandemic and heightened tension and polarization, both in the country and in congregations.

Just months later, in October 2021, the alarm bell grew louder as that percentage climbed to 38 percent—that is, nearly two in five pastors now admit they are thinking about walking away from full-time ministry.[6]

Though these worrying numbers are specific to senior pastors, the strain of ministry is not exclusive to leaders at the top. In this study, too, Barna sees indications of burnout risk among children's ministry leaders. COVID-19 alone has affected their ability to lead (37% "a great deal," 38% "a fair amount"), and the data point to waning satisfaction.

Spiritual health and work-life balance are areas of particular concern for children's ministry leaders. Only 19 percent are completely satisfied with the former and 15 percent are completely satisfied with the latter.

Barna sees indications of burnout risk and waning satisfaction among children's ministry leaders

Over decades of research, Barna has consistently observed that pastors and church leaders tend toward optimism and are disinclined to select negative or seemingly "wrong" answers. The fact that 16 percent of children's ministry leaders express dissatisfaction with their work-life balance and the majority falls into middling levels of satisfaction at best should be taken seriously.

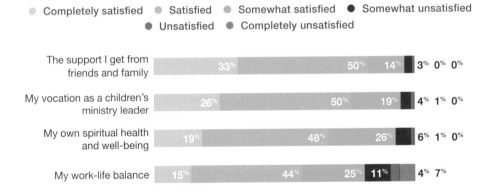

Children's ministry leaders:
Personally, how satisfied are you with each of the following . . . ?

● Completely satisfied   ● Satisfied   ● Somewhat satisfied   ● Somewhat unsatisfied
● Unsatisfied   ● Completely unsatisfied

The support I get from friends and family: 33% · 50% · 14% · 3% · 0% · 0%

My vocation as a children's ministry leader: 26% · 50% · 19% · 4% · 1% · 0%

My own spiritual health and well-being: 19% · 48% · 26% · 6% · 1% · 0%

My work-life balance: 15% · 44% · 25% · 11% · 4% · 7%

n=600 U.S. children's ministry leaders, June 8–August 16, 2021.

Cracks in the Kids' Ministry Support System

As we've covered earlier in this book, children's ministry leaders are convinced of the great importance of their calling and work, even seeing it as a key to church growth.

They aren't so sure that sentiment is shared by others. Rather, the slight majority agrees to some extent (15% strongly, 41% somewhat) that children's ministry is often forgotten in their church.

Children's ministry leaders: "Children's ministry is often forgotten in the church"

● Agree strongly   ● Agree somewhat

n=600 U.S. children's ministry leaders, June 8–August 16, 2021.

As a children's ministry leader, how satisfied are you with each of the following?

● Completely satisfied   ● Satisfied

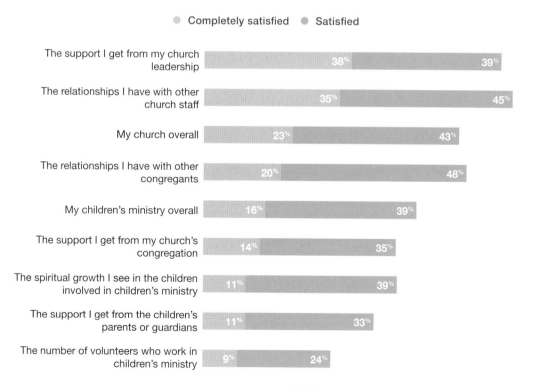

	Completely satisfied	Satisfied
The support I get from my church leadership	38%	39%
The relationships I have with other church staff	35%	45%
My church overall	23%	43%
The relationships I have with other congregants	20%	48%
My children's ministry overall	16%	39%
The support I get from my church's congregation	14%	35%
The spiritual growth I see in the children involved in children's ministry	11%	39%
The support I get from the children's parents or guardians	11%	33%
The number of volunteers who work in children's ministry	9%	24%

n=600 U.S. children's ministry leaders, June 8–August 16, 2021.

Children's Ministry Leaders Describe the Engagement Gap

At your church, how supportive are each of the following of the children's ministry? ● **Very supportive**
At your church, how engaged are each of the following in children's ministry? ● **Very engaged**

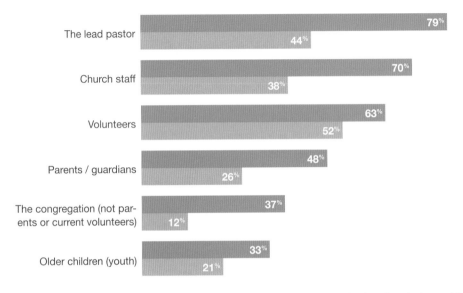

- The lead pastor — 79% / 44%
- Church staff — 70% / 38%
- Volunteers — 63% / 52%
- Parents / guardians — 48% / 26%
- The congregation (not parents or current volunteers) — 37% / 12%
- Older children (youth) — 33% / 21%

n=600 U.S. children's ministry leaders, June 8–August 16, 2021.

Do you feel that you have an adequate number of . . . ?

● Yes ● No

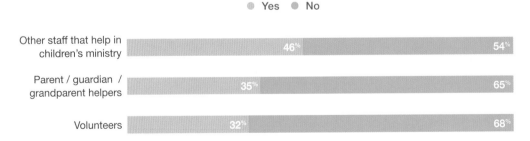

- Other staff that help in children's ministry — 46% / 54%
- Parent / guardian / grandparent helpers — 35% / 65%
- Volunteers — 32% / 68%

n=600 U.S. children's ministry leaders, June 8–August 16, 2021.

This is an indictment of how children's ministry can sometimes be treated like the "kid's table" of the congregation, rather than as a central component of the discipleship of the whole church.

Some children's ministry leaders' needs are not being adequately met or are perhaps being overlooked entirely. Leaders appear thankful for the support they do receive—and, at the same time, aware of the support they lack.

On the surface, children's ministry leaders tend to express moderate if not complete satisfaction with the support and relationships they have through leadership, staff and the church, and kids' ministry at large. Satisfaction dwindles when it comes to the support from the congregation, parents and guardians, and volunteers.

Digging a bit deeper, though, we can compare children's ministry leaders' assessment of the level of *support* vs. the actual level of *engagement* they observe from various parties. There are some puzzling gaps, especially concerning the involvement of the presumably supportive lead pastor and church staff, as well as parents and the congregation. It is possible children's ministry leaders are thinking of more general support that they don't categorize as "engagement," such as prayer, shared vision, church funds and so on. *None* of the stakeholder groups Barna asked about is seen as "very engaged" by a majority of children's ministry leaders.

Many of these leaders directly identify the deficit. About two-thirds of children's ministry leaders do not feel they have adequate numbers of church staff (65%) or parents, guardians and grandparents (68%) to help run the program.

Volunteers, often load-bearers in kids' ministries (see page 61), are the most involved support group and produce the smallest gap between perceived support and actual engagement (63% of leaders say they are "very supportive," 52% of leaders say they are "very engaged"). One-quarter of our sample of children's ministry leaders (25%) is serving in an unpaid, volunteer capacity themselves. In many ways, volunteers are the heartbeat of services and programs for kids. Still, more than half of children's ministry leaders (54%) say they don't have an adequate number of volunteers.

Overall, children's ministry leaders long for more support from all directions, especially from parents and guardians themselves (69%), as well as from the congregation at large (57%) and, of course, from volunteers (45%). Just one in 10 (10%) says, "I have all I need."

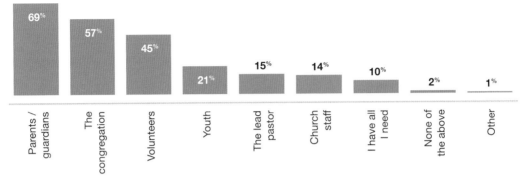

**"As a children's ministry leader,
I wish I were receiving more support from . . ."**

69% Parents / guardians

57% The congregation

45% Volunteers

21% Youth

15% The lead pastor

14% Church staff

10% I have all I need

2% None of the above

1% Other

n=600 U.S. children's ministry leaders, June 8–August 16, 2021.

Looking at where children's ministry leaders operate with a sense of authority, we see again some practical areas in which they feel they have little control. Though the majority of leaders feels they have "a great deal" of authority in many matters of children's ministry—like curriculum, program structure, facilities and so on—percentages slip most in two key areas: volunteers and budget.

Bigger is not necessarily better in children's ministry

Issues with support are about something more than dollar signs and sign-up sheets, however. Leading children's ministry in a larger and / or more-resourced church does mean having more authority over budget and volunteers, the data show—but it does not necessarily alleviate desires for greater support. Looking at categories of church size or church / ministry budget, there are few significant differences in children's ministry leaders' perceptions of the adequacy or level of support they receive. In fact, leaders with smaller churches and smaller budgets express *greater* contentment and satisfaction on some points, especially when it comes to support from the se-

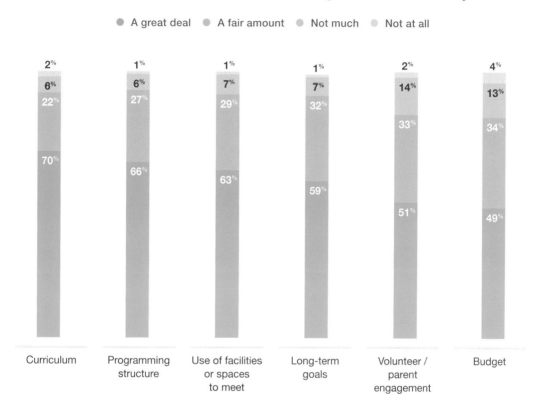

Children's ministry leaders: In your church, how much authority do feel you have over each of the following for children's ministry?

● A great deal   ● A fair amount   ● Not much   ● Not at all

	A great deal	A fair amount	Not much	Not at all
Curriculum	70%	22%	6%	2%
Programming structure	66%	27%	6%	1%
Use of facilities or spaces to meet	63%	29%	7%	1%
Long-term goals	59%	32%	7%	1%
Volunteer / parent engagement	51%	33%	14%	2%
Budget	49%	34%	13%	4%

n=600 U.S. children's ministry leaders, June 8–August 16, 2021.

nior pastor and church staff. And in larger churches, children's ministry leaders still describe a volunteer shortage.

Granted, children's ministry leaders in churches with more people or more money are more likely to express personal satisfaction in their ministry vocation. But their steadiness doesn't seem to guarantee stability in their program.

Are needs growing proportionate to the reach of the children's ministry? If the prevailing sense is that children's ministry is often forgotten by the church, do larger, busier churches present more for the kids' program to get lost behind? Is it possible that the quality and consistency of engagement and resources, rather than the quantity, are better indicators of adequate support? The research can't say for certain, though these are all likely scenarios. What's plain is that bigger is not necessarily better in children's ministry.

While this might be some encouragement to children's ministry leaders who wonder if they are flailing simply because they are in smaller or under-funded programs, it reveals that some deficits stem from widespread, even intangible problems that may need to be addressed by the Church at large. And it suggests that children's ministry leaders, and the teams and congregations they serve alongside, are still looking for the right measures of success.

A Confidence Crisis for Children's Ministry Leaders

Alongside inconsistent or inadequate support from the broader staff and church, children's ministry leaders are also facing insecurity. Specifically, they experience creeping doubt about their own influence, even as church-goers affirm it.

Parents and guardians are assumed to be the leading influence on children's *spiritual* development. After these primary caregivers, leaders in the church, including pastors, children's ministry leaders or volunteers, are seen as having great influence in children's faith formation.

This pattern might seem obvious, as parents benefit from proximity and quality time, and church leaders are explicitly spiritual figures and voices. Children's ministry leaders are most emphatic about the spiritual influence of both, including their own. But let's contrast this with the assumed impact of church and clergy in children's *general* development. There is little certainty among children's ministry leaders that churches are helping to shape children in these formative years. They seem to see their substantial spiritual influence as siloed from the broader set of influences in kids' formative years.

For the most part, children's ministry leaders and churched adults agree on the primary influences in kids' general development, with parents and guardians as well as friends topping the list.

Interesting deviations occur when it comes to the perceived role of the church and church leaders. Roughly two-fifths of churched adults, including

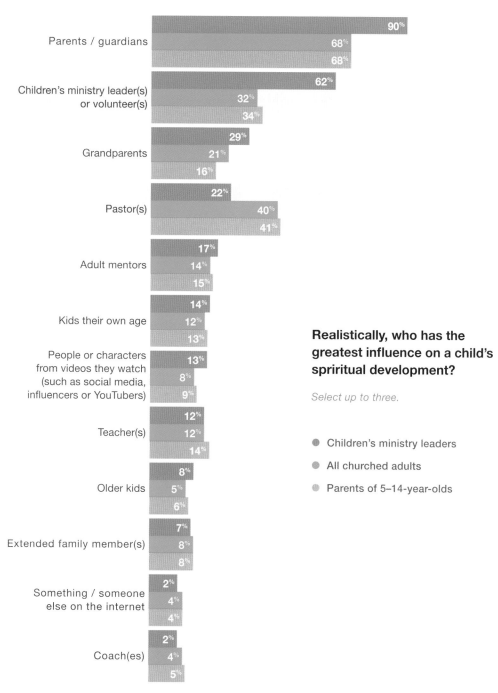

Parents / guardians — 90%, 68%, 68%

Children's ministry leader(s) or volunteer(s) — 62%, 32%, 34%

Grandparents — 29%, 21%, 16%

Pastor(s) — 22%, 40%, 41%

Adult mentors — 17%, 14%, 15%

Kids their own age — 14%, 12%, 13%

People or characters from videos they watch (such as social media, influencers or YouTubers) — 13%, 8%, 9%

Teacher(s) — 12%, 12%, 14%

Older kids — 8%, 5%, 6%

Extended family member(s) — 7%, 8%, 8%

Something / someone else on the internet — 2%, 4%, 4%

Coach(es) — 2%, 4%, 5%

Realistically, who has the greatest influence on a child's spriritual development?

Select up to three.

● Children's ministry leaders

● All churched adults

● Parents of 5–14-year-olds

n=600 U.S. children's ministry leaders, June 8–August 16, 2021;
n=2,051 U.S. churched adults, June 11–July 6, 2021;
n=1,021 U.S. churched adults with a child ages 5–14 at home, June 11–July 6, 2021.

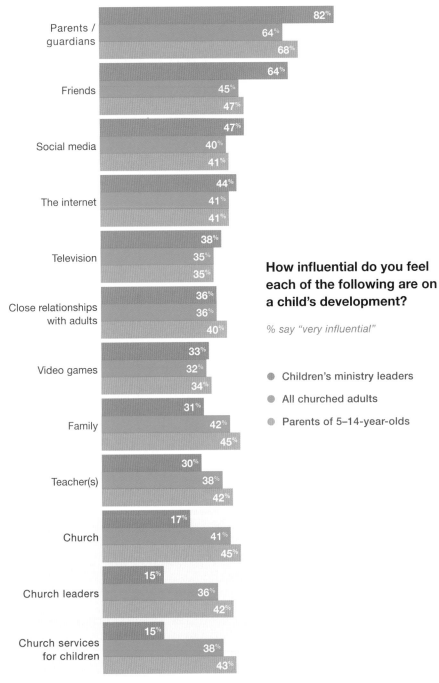

How influential do you feel each of the following are on a child's development?

% say "very influential"

- Children's ministry leaders
- All churched adults
- Parents of 5–14-year-olds

Parents / guardians — 82% / 64% / 68%
Friends — 64% / 45% / 47%
Social media — 47% / 40% / 41%
The internet — 44% / 41% / 41%
Television — 38% / 35% / 35%
Close relationships with adults — 36% / 36% / 40%
Video games — 33% / 32% / 34%
Family — 31% / 42% / 45%
Teacher(s) — 30% / 38% / 42%
Church — 17% / 41% / 45%
Church leaders — 15% / 36% / 42%
Church services for children — 15% / 38% / 43%

n=600 U.S. children's ministry leaders, June 8–August 16, 2021;
n=2,051 U.S. churched adults, June 11–July 6, 2021;
n=1,021 U.S. churched adults with a child ages 5–14 at home, June 11–July 6, 2021.

those with childrens-ministry-aged kids, say the church, church leaders and church services for kids are very influential on children. In the eyes of churched adults, the Church plays a significant part in children's development, either on par with or even more so than teachers, family and various forms of technology and media.

This feels like good news, right?

Yet however true churchgoers' perceptions may be, children's ministry leaders assume the church's influence is actually at the bottom of the list. Similar small proportions of children's ministry leaders call churches (17%), church leaders (15%) or children's ministry services (15%) "very" influential in children's development, consistently less than half the percentage of churched adults and parents who feel this way.

Children's ministry leaders seem to see their substantial spiritual influence as siloed from the broader set of influences in kids' formative years

Children's ministry leaders feel they are competing with—and falling behind—the influence of nearly every other input or relationship in kids' lives. Whatever input they might have in spiritual development specifically, it must not seem central or impactful enough to boost the church's place in a child's development at large. On top of that, either churchgoers are not sharing just how impactful they personally feel the church and children's ministry can be for kids, or children's ministry leaders are not in a place to believe or receive that kind of affirmation.

Some children's ministry leaders might need reminding that, regardless of their perceived deficits in resources and influence, they are already making a long-term difference—something churchgoers are very certain of (as we also covered on page 17). The opportunity is to better support and multiply that impact, and to involve more fellow disciples along the way.

In the concluding chapter of this book, we'll look at some of the ways the *whole* congregation can rally around the work of supporting children's ministry and helping kids grow into followers of Jesus. ●

REFLECTIONS

Process these questions on your own, with your team or with stakeholders in your children's ministry

- In your church, is there a gap between congregants' perceived importance of children's ministry and congregants' willingness to be involved in child discipleship?

- Outside the box of parents and guardians, who are some of those within your church who could volunteer with children's ministry if they were properly equipped?

- How is your church supporting the work-life balance, well-being and fulfillment of those leading or volunteering in children's ministry? What are some short-term and long-term changes that could encourage and equip them?

- What cultural or community influences most shape the kids in your church? Where would you place your children's ministry's influence by comparison?

- Consider your requests for children's ministry volunteers, and what it communicates about the purpose and the value of child discipleship. Are you simply asking people to get involved, or are you inviting volunteers and leaders to specifically help shape the next generation of disciples? Are you positioning it as a need for the ministry, for the kids or for the church at large? Do these requests occur relationally, in conversation, from the pulpit or only through bulletins, emails or forms? •

SPECIAL SECTION: A Profile of Children's Ministry Volunteers

On a weekly basis, volunteers and congregants play a versatile and crucial part in children's ministry services. Children's ministry leaders say adults in the church, other than staff, help with a wide range of activities: leading classes or teachings (60%), reading the Bible with kids (57%), leading songs and crafts (54%) or games (52%), engaging kids in meaningful conversations (49%) and more.

Overall, just over one-quarter of churched adults (28%) reports volunteering with their children's ministry, usually on a weekly basis (45%) or a few times a month (37%). Another 42 percent of churched adults say they used to volunteer in this program, while one in five who has never volunteered (21%) would be open to doing so.

It's perhaps no surprise that parents of children's-ministry-aged kids are more likely to volunteer (32%), being more hands-on in the activities and dimensions of their child's upbringing. This also means volunteers in older adult generations are increasingly rare. Only one in 10 churched Boomers (10%) currently volunteers in their church's ministry for children.

Other factors correlated with a greater likelihood of volunteering in children's ministry include more frequent church attendance and placing a high priority on children's ministry.

Typically, volunteers' activities center around the weekly service (74% of current and past volunteers say they helped in this program), though vacation Bible school (56%) and mid-week programs (34%) also require regular volunteer support.

> Children's ministry volunteers are a gritty minority; most are "very" committed to giving their time in this way

Twenty-eight percent of churched adults is a relatively small volunteer base, given how common and central the children's ministry is in U.S. churches, and given how much responsibility children's ministry leaders need volunteers to help shoulder on a weekly basis. But this is a gritty minority; most (78%) say they are "very" committed to giving their time in this way.

Children's ministry volunteers' reasons for participation are aligned with what both leaders and churched adults say is the primary objective of kids' ministry: They feel it is important to teach kids how to love and follow Jesus (49%). Other top reasons include believing today's children are the future of the church (44%) or feeling Christians have a responsibility to care for future generations (39%).

What holds back churched adults who have never volunteered in children's ministry? There is a wide range of barriers. At the top of the list, roughly one in five says they don't think they would be good at it (23%), they volunteer in other ways (23%), they haven't been asked (21%) or they simply don't have enough time (20%).

Broken down into specific activities, however, volunteering in children's ministry becomes more appealing. When all churched adults are asked, there is significant interest in volunteering for conversational, relational interactions through the children's ministry. Most activities garner at least some interest, with at least 40 percent being "very" interested in reading the Bible with kids (48%), sharing about their relationship with Jesus (45%), engaging kids in meaningful conversations (44%) or sharing about their personal faith journey (41%).

As churches and children's ministries make appeals to potential volunteers, it might be helpful to focus on the specifics of those needs and how they might foster meaningful interactions and relationships with the next generation. ●

Q&A: VOLUNTEERING FOR THE LONG HAUL

Q: Tell us your volunteer story. When did you come to your church? When did you begin to volunteer in children's ministry? What prompted that decision and did you feel "called" to do so? What did you see as the value of that time?

A: My husband and I came to Tri-City Bible Church in August of 1976. We had worked in Awana at First Baptist Church in San Clemente from 1974 to 1976. That had been my first time working in children's ministry, though I also spent some time as the nursery director.

I enjoy being around children, and I was truly excited about serving in this ministry. This was also an opportunity for my husband and I to do ministry together. When we were approached about serving in the kids' ministry, we said yes. As we had children at the time, we worked in ministry as a family.

Serving in children's ministry has changed my life. I love the Awana ministry. It has grown me as a Christian. Through this opportunity, I learned to teach lessons. Prior to this experience, I would never have thought I could teach lessons or direct other volunteers.

Q: How would you encourage people who don't presently have kids in the children's ministry to be involved? Why should they consider being a participant in the formation of faith and relationships with the next generation in their church? What are some misconceptions about this type of volunteering that you think could be corrected?

MAUREEN COOPER

Originally from Pittsburgh, Maureen met her husband Fred at First Baptist of Van Nuys after moving to Los Angeles. The two were married in 1972 before moving to San Clemente where they first got involved with Awana. Through their years of raising a family together—two sons and two daughters—Maureen and Fred continued serving in Awana and also in the children's ministry at their church. Fred passed away in 2014, having faithfully and lovingly served the children in his community for many decades. Maureen continues to serve in Awana today and currently holds the title of co-ministry director.

A: I would encourage people who don't have kids in the children's ministry to think about how serving in this ministry can impact kids' lives. They can become a mentor to these children. If they are seeking to serve somewhere, and there is a need in the kids' ministry, that could be the right place for them to serve. Children like to have, and are encouraged by, relationships with people who show they care.

Some people have misconceptions about serving in children's ministries because they think they have to be able to teach a lesson or be in charge of other volunteers or the entire classroom of kids. Children's ministry leaders should be very clear that volunteers serving in kids' ministry need only to do what they are comfortable with. The ministry should be explained clearly so that volunteers know what is expected of them and what their responsibilities will be.

> "Children's ministry leaders should be clear that volunteers serving in kids' ministry need only do what they are comfortable with"

People can also think that once they start volunteering for a ministry, they have to do it forever. That is not the case, and should be explained so that does not become a hindrance for them.

Q: Have there been times you have left or debated leaving your volunteer post in the children's ministry? If so, why? What helped you to stay or persevere?

A: I've loved this ministry from the very beginning. Throughout my time volunteering, I have never wanted to not serve in some capacity.

I feel that if the Lord wants me to stop serving, he would let me know. Until then, I will continue to serve.

Q: Can you share a story of seeing the rewards of your long-term volunteering with children's ministry?

A: One testimony that I see whenever I serve is that we have several former Awana club members, as well as their children, who now serve in the ministry.

Q: How do you think churches can better support children's ministry leaders and volunteers? What are the needs, pain points or hopes that you think need to be addressed in local churches to better invest in children's ministry and the next generation?

> "It is extremely difficult to recruit from the pulpit. It is much better to recruit face-to-face."

A: There are a number of things that come to mind here. The first is that children's ministry is often not given much priority, but I feel that churches definitely need to give it a higher priority.

We also need godly Christian men and women to step up and serve in children's ministry. It is extremely difficult to recruit from the pulpit. It is much better to recruit face-to-face. If a children's ministry leader or other church staff recognize someone who seems able to take on a leadership role, ask them if they'd have an interest in serving in the children's ministry.

I believe better training would help to give volunteers more confidence when they serve.

Lastly, I also think churches should utilize high-schoolers to serve in children's ministry. It is good training for them and allows them to be invested from a leadership standpoint while they invest in the lives of the younger children they're serving. ●

Q&A: SUPPORT & SOUL CARE FOR CHILDREN'S MINISTRY LEADERS

CYNTHIA DIXSON

Cynthia is a recognized children's ministry leader who has been an advocate for discipling children and youth for over 25 years. She currently serves as the children's ministry director at Oak Cliff Bible Fellowship Church, under the leadership of Dr. Tony Evans. As director, Cynthia's goal is to ensure that each child who attends one of her children's ministry programs become a life-long follower of Jesus Christ through the power of the gospel. Cynthia is married to her husband Dale. Together, they have four children and four grandchildren.

Q: The majority of children's ministry leaders agrees at least somewhat that children's ministry is often forgotten in the church. Meanwhile, leaders' satisfaction with their work-life balance and spiritual health is waning. Why might it be difficult for them to get the support they need and what should soul care for the children's ministry leader look like? How can the church and congregation better show up or indicate support?

A: I see this a lot here in this ministry. I've served in places where the children's ministries seem like the forgotten ministry.

Often, churches' first priority is to get the adults in seats, as kids might follow automatically. But this overlooks the reality of needing to invest in the future—the next generation is actually the most important thing we need to invest in.

Children's ministry leaders can also feel like they're pouring so much into discipling these kids, and they wonder if they will get to see a return on the investment, because investments in kids don't always show immediately. Often, investments are seen years down the line for kids' ministry.

I have had to *not* focus on looking for an investment, and instead focus on the larger picture: We plant the seed, we water the seed, and God gets to the increase. This is something I encourage my volunteers in. Mindset and expectations are very important to helping deter burnout.

There are other ways to deter burnout, including proper organization and structure of the kids' ministry. Honesty is also important—we need to be honest with our leadership. It's crucial to let them know if the ministry or people in the ministry are struggling and to ask for help and support.

We need volunteers for the long haul. I'm a big believer in self-care. It's OK to say no when you see a need arise—that need may be an opportunity for someone else to get involved in the ministry. It's also OK to say that you need to rest.

Q: What can be done to help increase engagement in children's ministry when leaders don't feel they have enough helping hands? How should children's ministries focus their efforts, even when resources and support are in short supply?

A: I would encourage children's ministry leaders to assess their ministry. My approach is to write a vision of what I see. I then put everything that's working well for us and what's not working well in side-by-side columns. When it comes to what's not working well, not having enough volunteers and not having enough budget are at the top of every list, always.

As I mentioned earlier, it's important to speak with your senior leadership and be honest about what is really going on in your ministry. Take initiative to outline what's going on in your children's ministry and come up with workable solutions to these issues.

After you do all that, have the pastor lead the campaign, reminding the church that they should be all about kids and the next generation.

Once you identify your biggest needs in your ministry and there is a plan to help meet these needs, start to dream big. Pray for those needs to be met in abundance. For example, if you're a small ministry and you only see 15 kids weekly, look in your vision and say, "I see this ministry having 100 kids." Go ahead and prepare for the 100 kids. Prepare for the harvest.

Q: Leaders feel they're competing with or even falling behind the influence of nearly every other input or relationship in kids' lives. What do you see as potential threats to the influence or effectiveness of a children's ministry in today's culture?

A: A threat to children's ministry is people giving up hope. They see the world and think, "How can we compete? What can we do when the world has so much influence?"

Never give up hope and never let the outside world influence your thinking on the effectiveness of discipling children toward Christ. Always have the confidence to know that we serve a risen Savior and Christ is in control of everything. You may feel inadequate, but sharing a smile or being kind to a child can be enough sometimes.

"All we can do is what God has called us to do, and that's to plant the seed"

Showing Christ doesn't mean you have to know every scripture in the Bible. It can simply be to know the kindness and goodness of Christ and live that out as a testimony daily.

We don't know the conversations God is having with the children we're serving. All we can do is what God has called us to do, and that's to plant the seed. He will take care of who waters the seed and he will take care of the harvest.

Q: Parents and guardians actually do believe children's ministry is making a long-term impact. What can churches and parents do to help boost children's ministry leaders' confidence in their influence in the lives of the children they serve?

A: Tell them thank you. It is that simple. "Thank you" goes a long way for me and for anybody else. When you pass by the children's ministry leader, tell them, "I see you, I see what you're doing for my child, and I see that you love my child." People want to know that they're appreciated, loved and thanked.

Parents should also be supportive. When the pastor says, "We need to do this for the kids' ministry ..." be there to support them—show up and be the rallying call.

Be their support system. Be there for them. Be their advocate. Be the first one to say, "They need more supplies. They need more resources. What can we do, pastor? What can we do to give our leaders the tools and resources they need to be successful?" Show up for them. ●

CHAPTER 4

REINFORCEMENTS FOR RESILIENCE

Are meaningful, intergenerational connections a key to sustaining the future Church?

In many churches, a congregation's first introduction to a child might be through a ceremony for a baby dedication, blessing or baptism. Typically, this involves some sort of commitment from congregants, perhaps through a charge, a reading or prayer. Churchgoers are called upon to be partners in the spiritual journey of the child and to be a faithful support to the parents and family.

Most Christians likely have a memory of being present for such a service or sacrament. Perhaps they nodded, repeated the liturgy or blessed the parent and child in passing. But how many went on to intentionally live out that commitment? To treat a child as an important part of the church community? To help draw a young disciple closer to God, and also to learn from their childlike faith?

Barna strategically broadened the scope of our survey beyond just those with a child in a kids' ministry program and invited the *whole* Church into this study—asking churched adults in general to weigh in on the state of child discipleship today.

Our ability to hear from churchgoers—parents and non-parents alike—in this study doesn't just satisfy our curiosity. The data suggest the faithful presence and meaningful participation of congregants can be crucial in coming alongside ministers and parents, addressing gaps in children's ministries and nurturing resilient faith in young and old alike.

Invitations for Involvement

Churched adults have different ideas about how an individual should engage with children's ministry relative to age, stage or occupation. About half believe the involvement of parents (52%) is "expected," alongside the senior pastor (50%) and church staff (48%). For other groups, however, the plurality of churched adults assumes engagement is "encouraged but not expected." This is true whether referring to the involvement of older children / youth (45%), young adults (46%), middle-aged adults (49%) or seniors (43%) in the church. One in five churched adults (18%) goes so far as to say senior congregants are neither encouraged nor expected to engage in kids' ministry.

> ## Understanding and facilitating intergenerational relationships can be a worthwhile investment in the future of the Church

If these seem like low expectations, know that churched adults might be taking their cues from the heads of the program—one-quarter of whom neither encourages nor expects participation, even from their senior pastor or ministry colleagues. In fact, children's ministry leaders are less likely than congregants to say they "expect" involvement from anyone on the list.

Of course, we know these are some of the same groups children's ministry leaders wish for more support from, pointing to ambivalent attitudes among leaders as they struggle to build up their program. The reality is children's ministry leaders aren't sure the adults in their church are all that interested in involvement in children's ministry. One-quarter (24%) says most or all of the adults in their church are "willing to engage with children," while the majority of leaders (56%) feels only some adults have this willingness.

Just One Loving, Caring Adult

All told, children's ministry leaders are unsure of the value of kids interacting with and having relationships with other churchgoing adults (as noted on page 22 and 58). As an outcome or measure of discipleship, they don't discount it, but they don't necessarily prioritize it.

At your church, how are the following groups invited to be involved in children's ministry?

Base: churched adults whose church has a children's ministry

● Children's ministry leaders   ● Churched adults

| Expected | Encouraged but not expected | Not encouraged or expected | Not sure |

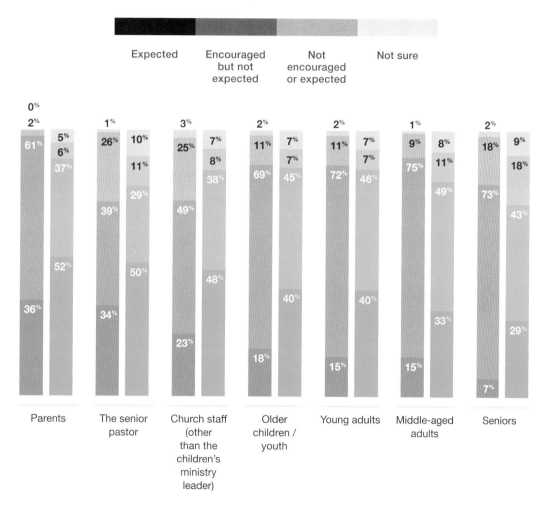

Parents
0%
2%
61% / 5%
6%
37%
36% / 52%

The senior pastor
1%
26% / 10%
11%
39% / 29%
34% / 50%

Church staff (other than the children's ministry leader)
3%
25% / 7%
8%
49% / 38%
23% / 48%

Older children / youth
2%
11% / 7%
7%
69% / 45%
18% / 40%

Young adults
2%
11% / 7%
7%
72% / 46%
15% / 40%

Middle-aged adults
1%
9% / 8%
11%
75% / 49%
15% / 33%

Seniors
2%
18% / 9%
18%
73% / 43%
7% / 29%

n=600 U.S. children's ministry leaders, June 8–August 16, 2021;
n=1,643 U.S. churched adults whose church has a children's ministry, June 11–July 6, 2021.

Children's ministry leaders: Thinking about the adults in your church congregation, how many fit the following description: *willing to engage with children?*

All ● Most ● Some ● Few ● None

| 5% | 19% | 56% | 19% | 1% |

n=600 U.S. children's ministry leaders, June 8–August 16, 2021.

Is this a missed opportunity? This study suggests that understanding and facilitating intergenerational relationships can be a worthwhile investment in the future of the Church.

Today, two in five churched parents of 5–14-year-olds (39%) indicate their child has a meaningful relationship with an adult at their church. Specifically, these adults say their child has a positive, meaningful relationship with another adult at church and also say it's "completely true" their child has a meaningful relationship with a mentoring adult through their church.

Two in Five Children in Children's Ministry Have a Meaningful Relationship with an Adult

● Yes ● No

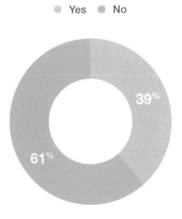

n=1,021 U.S. churched adults with a child ages 5–14 at home, June 11–July 6, 2021.

Opportunities to form strong connections between churchgoing adults and kids increase with both regular church attendance as well as attendance in smaller churches, perhaps a reflection of the consistency, proximity and intimacy of such worship environments. These kinds of relationships might seem like a natural byproduct of simply being a part of a church community. However, Barna's research, in both this and previous studies, urges that intergenerational community be embraced with intention.

Children who have a meaningful relationship with an adult at church are more likely to be rooted in scripture

In Barna's *Households of Faith* study, produced in partnership with Lutheran Hour Ministries, we observed an interesting pattern among practicing Christian families: Hospitality and spiritual vibrancy go hand in hand. Specifically, when households regularly host non-family guests, several other positive activities are also common: shared Bible-reading, faith conversations and other fun recreational activities.[7] When neighbors, friends and fellow churchgoers are welcomed as an extension of both one's faith and one's household, it bears spiritual fruit across parties and generations.

Additionally, David Kinnaman and Mark Matlock's research for *Faith for Exiles* showed that resilient disciples tend to have strong relational networks. Within faith communities, resilient disciples reported strong ties, even across generations.[8] They indicated having close adult friends at church during their childhood and described church as a place where they belonged and felt encouraged and emotionally close to others.

This was also true in dimensions that didn't have an exclusive orientation to faith. For instance, resilient disciples were more likely than their peers to have close, trusted friends with whom they exchanged secrets, advice and honesty, helping each other be better people. In multiple ways, resilience is linked with being more connected, more rooted and having qualitatively stronger friendships.

Likewise, in this study, we see time and again that a child having even one meaningful relationship with an adult through their church connects to a slew of other positive experiences and behaviors rooted in discipleship. Keep in mind: (1) these are correlative not causal trends, (2) we are using parents' perspectives as a proxy for the experiences of their children, and (3) these are still young people in early, formative years of life. Yet, even acknowledging the limits of this vantage point, it's clear that faithful relationships across age groups and beyond the household help people come to know who they are in Christ, in the Church and in community.

First, we see that children who have a meaningful relationship with an adult at church are more likely to be **rooted in scripture.** Whether memorizing verses, beginning to grasp biblical narratives and principles or embarking on independent study and application, parents of

Parents of 5–14 year-olds: Thinking about your child and their experience at church, how true are the following about them?

"My child ..."
% say "completely true"

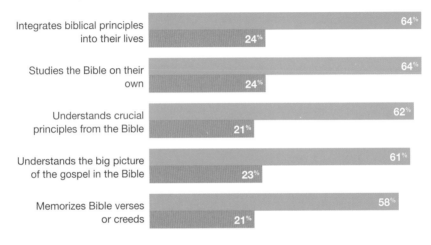

● Child has a meaningful adult relationship   ● Child does not have a meaningful adult relationship

Integrates biblical principles into their lives	64% / 24%
Studies the Bible on their own	64% / 24%
Understands crucial principles from the Bible	62% / 21%
Understands the big picture of the gospel in the Bible	61% / 23%
Memorizes Bible verses or creeds	58% / 21%

n=1,021 U.S. churched adults with a child ages 5–14 at home, June 11–July 6, 2021.

5–14-year-olds who have intergenerational support report seeing deep engagement with the Bible.

These kids also seem to be **grounded in children's ministry and the life of the church** in general, their parents report. When children have a meaningful, mentoring relationship with an adult, they are more likely than their peers to be enthusiastic about services. We see a spike in participation in (or, at least, availability of) various spiritual or recreational activities in a children's ministry. Kids with an anchoring adult relationship at church are also anchored in the whole worship experience, being more likely to join in everything from prayer to play.

Finally, parents' responses indicate that, when kids are in healthy, intergenerational Christian community, they externalize their faith and **move toward generous, countercultural behavior.** Three-quarters of parents

Parents of 5–14-year-olds:
Thinking about how your children interact with church and children's ministry, how much would you agree or disagree with the following?

% strongly agree

● Child has a meaningful adult relationship ● Child does not have a meaningful adult relationship

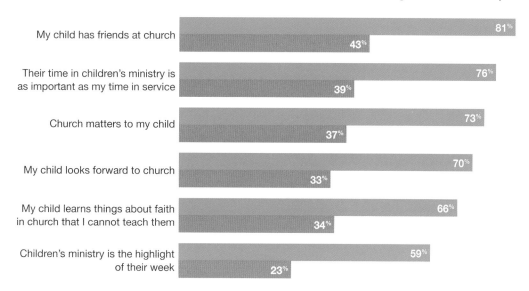

My child has friends at church — 81% / 43%

Their time in children's ministry is as important as my time in service — 76% / 39%

Church matters to my child — 73% / 37%

My child looks forward to church — 70% / 33%

My child learns things about faith in church that I cannot teach them — 66% / 34%

Children's ministry is the highlight of their week — 59% / 23%

n=1,021 U.S. churched adults with a child ages 5–14 at home, June 11–July 6, 2021.

of children with such connections say it's "completely true" their church gives their child an opportunity to understand their gifts, contribute, feel like part of a team and engage today's culture with love.

Among parents whose child doesn't have a positive, meaningful relationship with an adult at church, nearly half (46%) say they would like for this to be the case. One-third (33%) says they aren't sure, indicating some uncertainty about what such a relationship might look like or with whom their child might have such a relationship. These parents might need some examples, reassurance or coaching from peers or leaders.

Or they might just need some introductions. This could be difficult in churches where programs are siloed, or volunteer numbers are low.

Remember (see page 62), children's ministry volunteers' reasons for participation include feeling it is important to teach kids how to love and follow

Parents of 5–14-year-olds:
At church, how often does your child do each of the following?

% say "weekly"

● Child has a meaningful adult relationship   ● Child does not have a meaningful adult relationship

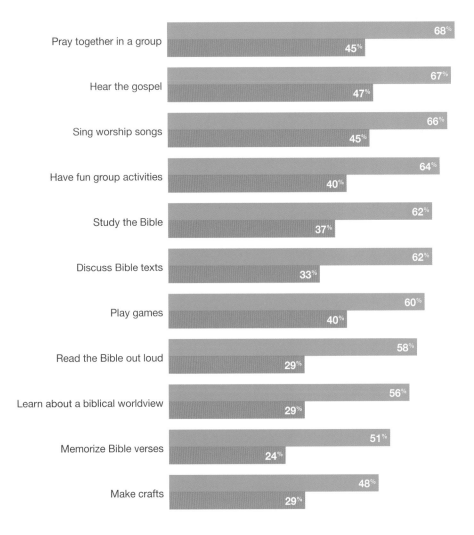

Pray together in a group — 68% / 45%
Hear the gospel — 67% / 47%
Sing worship songs — 66% / 45%
Have fun group activities — 64% / 40%
Study the Bible — 62% / 37%
Discuss Bible texts — 62% / 33%
Play games — 60% / 40%
Read the Bible out loud — 58% / 29%
Learn about a biblical worldview — 56% / 29%
Memorize Bible verses — 51% / 24%
Make crafts — 48% / 29%

n=1,021 U.S. churched adults with a child ages 5–14 at home, June 11–July 6, 2021.

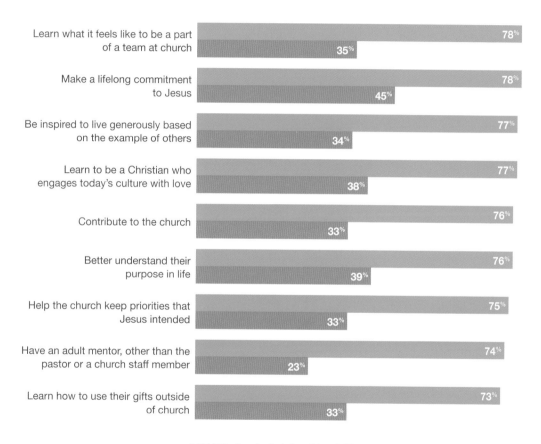

**Parents of 5–14-year-olds:
At church, my child has the opportunity to . . .”**

% say "completely true"

● Child has a meaningful adult relationship   ● Child does not have a meaningful adult relationship

Learn what it feels like to be a part of a team at church	35%	78%
Make a lifelong commitment to Jesus	45%	78%
Be inspired to live generously based on the example of others	34%	77%
Learn to be a Christian who engages today's culture with love	38%	77%
Contribute to the church	33%	76%
Better understand their purpose in life	39%	76%
Help the church keep priorities that Jesus intended	33%	75%
Have an adult mentor, other than the pastor or a church staff member	23%	74%
Learn how to use their gifts outside of church	33%	73%

n=1,021 U.S. churched adults with a child ages 5–14 at home, June 11–July 6, 2021.

Jesus (49%), believing today's children are the future of the church (44%) or feeling Christians have a responsibility to care for future generations (39%). Could these be galvanizing messages your church could share with congregants and potential volunteers?

Strong networks of old and young Christians don't just happen by accident

Additionally, the holdups for churchgoers who don't volunteer with kids include the fear of not being good at it and simply not being asked. How are adults of all ages being equipped to "pass down" faith and to feel at ease in intergenerational interactions? Are churches neglecting the very first step: to directly ask churched adults to engage in discipleship of and community with the next generation?

Strong networks of old and young Christians don't just happen by accident. Likely, in the charts you just reviewed, we see more than the fruit of adults and children connecting in their walk with Jesus. We also see the reward of resilient guardians who placed value on attendance in the first place. We see the success of churches and children's ministries that strived to take kids seriously and created environments and services that nurtured young faith and welcomed wisdom from elders. These charts are colored with the decisions and experiences of an entire church community, pronounced in the meaningful connection of two Christ-followers across generations. ●

REFLECTIONS

Process these questions on your own, with your team or with stakeholders in your children's ministry

- How are you ensuring that kids in your congregation are experiencing an engaged community of care, even beyond Sunday programs?

- In what specific activities or areas would you welcome more congregants to share the weight and blessing of child discipleship?

- What can your ministry do to equip, support and include others as influencers of kids in your congregation, especially those who might typically hang back or who don't have kids in children's ministry at the moment?

- How can the senior leadership of your congregation make it clear that child discipleship is a responsibility and outcome for the church at large?

- Who were some of the loving, caring adults involved in your own discipleship?

LACY FINN BORGO, DMIN

Lacy teaches and provides spiritual direction for various organizations in spiritual formation and spiritual direction, including Renovaré, Fuller Theological Seminary, Portland Seminary, The Companioning Center and Mercy Center, Burlingame. Lacy has a spiritual direction and supervision of spiritual directors ministry for adults, and provides spiritual direction for children at Haven House, a transitional facility for families without homes in Olathe, Colorado. Her book *Spiritual Conversations with Children: Listening to God Together* was released March 2020. Her children's book *All Will Be Well* will be released in the Fall of 2022. You can find her at www.GoodDirtMinistries.org.

Q&A:
COMMUNITY-BUILDING FOR RESILIENT DISCIPLESHIP

Q: How would you encourage churchgoers—whether or not they presently have kids in the children's ministry—to be involved? Why should they consider being a participant in the formation of faith and relationships with the next generation in their church?

A: Perhaps the first area that could use attention is the reciprocal nature of spiritual formation. Separating children's spiritual growth from adults' spiritual growth has not served us well. What is good for the child's relationship with God is good for the adult's relationship with God. I can't tell you the number of adults who are touched deeply by the children's sermon each week. There are gifts for our life with God that can only be released by being with children. It might also help to integrate children into the main rhythms of the church. Children need to be a visible and vital part of what any church is doing. This is not only to help adults see kids as essential but also for children to know that they are essential. Children need to feel ownership for the Church body.

Q: Kids who grow up in the church *and* choose to stay tend to say they had meaningful connections to adults in the congregation during their childhood. Have you experienced or witnessed this? Why do you think this might be?

A: It is true in every way. When adults invest in the lives of children, bonds are made that extend to people both within and outside the church. The past, present and future of the Church are found in relationships, not institutions or buildings. With the religious and political shifts going on in the Western world, relationships will hold even if the institutions or buildings do not.

Adults need to be growing in how to be in healthy relationships with children and adolescents. In this shifting time in our cultural history, adults need to trust that God can be found and is at work in the upcoming generation. Adults must learn to see through the eyes of the Spirit rather than the old patterns to which individuals might be attached.

> "If we are about the work of deepening relationships with God and not merely keeping an institution alive, we will need to invest in relationships with children"

Intergenerational relationships are a gift of the Spirit that knock off petrified ways of being that no longer serve individuals' lives with God. They also help to guide (through a listening presence and a rare word fitly spoken) the new generation into the new thing God might be doing.

Q: Outside of services, what are some topics, activities or opportunities you would encourage congregations to embrace to invite more "cross" (cross-generational, cross-cultural, etc.) relationships to form? What kind of impact does this have on faith? What are the challenges of these types of relationships across differences—and how would you encourage churchgoers to navigate those?

A: This is a chance to dream.

What if a church set up a listening center, peopled by adults who are willing to listen to children and teens who need a loving, listening presence? Being a listening presence to a child will help them to hear themselves and give them a safe space to share. We all need this. It will also shape the image of God for the child. The picture of God that each of us has is shaped by those adults in our lives who loved us well. Wholehearted listening is an act of love.

How about an intergenerational movie or music night where adults, children and adolescents watch a movie together or listen to music and then discuss where they experienced goodness, beauty and truth? This could be a place of great challenge. It can be hard for adults to engage with the shifting culture and engage with how children are processing it. It causes fear to rise. But it is also an opportunity for the children to be known and for the faith of an adult to be challenged to trust more deeply.

If we are about the work of deepening relationships with God and not merely keeping an institution alive, we will need to invest in relationships with children and adolescents.

All of us grow in our relationship with God and others through encounters. If we want to disciple children, we must encounter them wholeheartedly with vulnerability and honesty in the spaces where they live and play. In this way, we can help children recognize and respond to God wherever they are. Encounters build connection with God and community, which is a major characteristic of resilience. ●

Children's Ministry Matters— Now What?

For church communities to cultivate lasting faith among the next generation, a variety of individuals and relationships must be engaged. As we conclude this report, let's review some of the primary participants and stakeholders in children's ministry and what the research reveals about their needs and opportunities.

Whether you fall into one of these groups or have influence with them, use these reflection questions and takeaways to inspire and sustain child discipleship in a new reality.

Insight for Church Leadership:
Get aligned on the vision and the metrics for effectiveness of children's ministry.

You and your team likely don't need convincing that child discipleship is important; Barna's research shows nearly unanimous agreement on this point, from the pulpit to the pew. Still, the data suggest senior leadership's expressed support of children's ministry exceeds their actual engagement. Leaders may need to be more intentional to make sure the ministry clearly reflects that sense of importance—in communicating vision, allocating resources and monitoring impact.

If 89 percent of children's ministry leaders are correct that churches cannot grow without effective children's ministry, the church at large must be able to understand and measure child discipleship holistically and accurately. As it stands, half of children's ministry leaders feel it's difficult to evaluate their impact.

Barna CEO David Kinnaman writes in *The State of Your Church*, "When we talk about measuring what matters, we must keep these principles in mind: 1) Success in God's economy is faithfulness; 2) some things, especially in the realm of spirituality, are very hard to measure; 3) many things can—and should—be measured; 4) big can be great, but bigger is not always better; 5) when things look bleak, God can still be working; 6) we need to be willing to stop what we're doing and go in a different direction, and 7) even as we develop a theology of success, we need a theology of failure."[9]

How can your team take these principles and determine or refine common goals and metrics for child discipleship on a local level? What does leadership currently value in children's ministry—attendance? Adult-to-child ratio? Signs that kids are learning or having fun? Are there additional or more important metrics to measure what matters most?

Insight for Children's Ministry Leader & Volunteers:
Do not grow weary in doing good.

The psychologist Herbert J. Freudenberger is credited with providing the technical definition of "burnout," which he explained as a combination of emotional exhaustion, a depleted ability to care and a decreased sense of accomplishment.[10]

Collectively, children's ministry leaders show signs of all three in Barna's research. They describe feeling unsure of their long-term impact, fearing that kids will walk away from the faith and not knowing how to gauge their effectiveness. Their work-life balance is at risk. They often feel siloed from the rest of the church and ministry or like they don't have what they need to do a job they see as very important. "I'm afraid of getting it wrong," 37 percent of children's ministry leaders tell Barna. These insecurities persist even though parents and guardians attest to the long-term impact of children's ministries.

Several approaches could help close the gaps in children's ministry leaders' confidence and energy for their sacred work.

In the priorities and communication of your senior leadership, is there inclusion and affirmation of children's ministries? In the daily lives (and especially the weekend routines) of your children's ministry leaders, is there room for soul-care, connection and counsel? Are children's ministry leaders and volunteers truly trained for the profound responsibility of child discipleship? Are they given agency to lead and disciple out of their strengths and to focus their planning and energy efficiently? If not, what conversations need to be had or what resources need to be provided to better invest in this group of leaders? Are church methods for recruiting and equipping the help of volunteers in need of refreshment and restructuring? Finally, are there strong assessment or feedback loops, allowing the leadership and church to know how children's ministry leaders are really doing and allowing children's ministry leaders to see and learn from the fruit of their work?

Insight for Parents, Guardians & Caregivers:
Champion children's ministries and embrace your influence.

Biblically and pragmatically, it makes sense that parents and guardians take a lead role in the discipleship of their own children. That's a message that has been widely accepted and communicated in churches and children's ministries—but it hasn't necessarily been well-implemented.

Meanwhile, Christian parents and guardians put a *lot* of trust in churches, celebrate their impact and look to them to address tough topics with kids. They tell Barna that a kid's experience and an adult's experience of a Sunday service are equally important. These caregivers are well-positioned to be cheerleaders of and participants in local children's ministries—yet they also risk being over-reliant on children's ministry leaders and volunteers (who, as mentioned previously, have limitations of their own) and shirking their Monday–Saturday spiritual influence.

The reality is Christian parents can't do everything for child discipleship, *and* churches can't do everything for child discipleship. These partners in the faith formation of the next generation must bring their best *and* expect the best of the other.

How can your church show up with relevant resources and relationships intended to support weekday and household discipleship? Hybrid and digital ministry, especially through the pandemic era, have further complicated this exchange between churches and families—are those factors being accounted for, and how are new opportunities and mediums for discipleship being stewarded? How can households and churches begin to navigate their spiritual investment in children as something that is dynamic and interconnected, not something shrugged off or passed to the other party when hours, resources, knowledge or confidence are in short supply?

In a time when both corporate worship and individual discipleship face external pressures, it's crucial to move past internal finger-pointing when young people walk away from the Church and instead shoulder up to the shared task of passing on resilient faith.

Insight for Churchgoers:
Community-building is a key to cultivating lasting faith—and you have a part to play.

More than half of children's ministry leaders feel that children's ministry is often forgotten in the church. Understandably, they temper their expectations for the interest and engagement of churchgoers.

Yet one of the most valuable findings in this study is that children who engage with other mentoring adults who care for and disciple them have remarkably different experiences of faith. They are growing roots in the church and in scripture. They are included, valued members of the community, seen and encouraged in their purpose.

How is your church setting up the *whole* congregation—not just the parents or the "usual suspects" (who could clearly use some support and solidarity!)—to care about and see their role in forming the faith of children? Most churches are likely encouraging adults toward sharing their faith through evangelism, contributing their gifts generously or growing in discipleship community—could these disciplines be framed within the context of intergenerational community, not just peer-to-peer relationships? What sermons, groups, events or opportunities nurture interest in volunteering with kids or strike up mentoring relationships? How do even the little weekly moments—in services, small groups, church lobbies and so on—recognize the presence and the faith of children and integrate them within the culture of the whole church? How can every member of your church identify what they might have to give to the next generation?

Part of being disciplers of children means being equippers of adults.

Insight for Children:
"Jesus loves me, this I know."

These lyrics are often among the first lessons children learn through their church. This message is also the main one that leaders, parents, volunteers and congregants believe a child should take with them when they age out of children's ministry: Nearly all leaders and the strong majority of churched adults and parents strongly agrees that active engagement in a children's ministry should result in personally knowing Jesus' love.

What does it look like for the gospel to penetrate the minds and hearts of young people, for the awareness of Jesus' love to survive the questions and pressures of adolescence and for Christ-likeness to shape the attitudes and behaviors of the next generation?

The bottom line: The U.S. Church risks seeing more young people walk away from the faith if it is not willing to reimagine its calling and approach to children's ministry.

Truly *knowing* Jesus' love requires more than memorizing phrases and having fun, more than building programs to attract and entertain (or edutain). Formation of young disciples is a holistic effort—holistic in the sense that it considers the whole person and their development, and holistic in the sense that it should involve multiple participants and mentors.

The Jesus that leaders and churchgoers hope children come to know drew kids near and admired their faith (Mark 10:13–16). He was vigilant about protecting them (Matthew 18:16–17). He blessed and shared their contributions to the community (John 6: 9–11).

To build the future of the Church and invest in a new generation of disciples, Christians are called to do the same. The door is open, the light is coming in—is your church willing to step out in faith, leave old realities and walk out a new vision for child discipleship? ●

Methodology

This study included a set of quantitative online surveys.

The first survey interviewed 2,051 U.S. adults who attended church at least once in the last six months. They were surveyed online between June 11–July 6, 2021, through a national consumer research panel. Included within the sample of churched adults is an oversample of 1,021 parents with children between the ages of 5 and 14 years old. The data has been statistically weighted by age, gender, race / ethnicity, income, education, region and parenting. The estimated margin of error is +/- 1.8%.

Additionally, Barna surveyed 600 U.S. Protestant church leaders who indicate they have decision-making responsibility for their church's children's ministry. Within this sample, 481 leaders are specifically on-staff children's pastors, on-staff youth pastors or volunteer children's leaders, and 119 leaders are senior pastors who don't have a children's ministry leader. For recruitment, Barna Group reached out to senior protestant pastors through Barna's Pastor Panel and asked them to forward the invitation to whomever is responsible for children's ministry in their church. The data has been statistically weighted by church size, region and denomination. The estimated margin of error is +/- 2.5%. ●

Endnotes

1. Barna Group, "Research Shows That Spiritual Maturity Process Should Start at a Young Age," November 17, 2003, https://www.barna.com/research/research-shows-that-spiritual-maturity-process-should-start-at-a-young-age/.
2. Andy Crouch, *The Tech-Wise Family* (Grand Rapids, MI: Baker Books, 2017).
3. David Kinnaman and Mark Matlock, *Faith for Exiles* (Grand Rapids, MI: Baker Books, 2019).
4. Barna Group, *Faith Leadership in a Divided Culture*, (Ventura, CA: Barna Group, 2019) 71.
5. Barna Group, "38% of U.S. Pastors Have Thought About Quitting Full-Time Ministry in the Past Year," November 16, 2021, https://www.barna.com/research/pastors-well-being/.
6. Barna, "38% of US Pastors."
7. Barna Group, *Households of Faith*, (Ventura, CA: Barna Group, 2019).
8. Kinnaman and Matlock, *Faith for Exiles*.
9. Barna Group, *The State of Your Church*, (Ventura, CA: Barna Group, 2022) 15.
10. Herbert J. Freudenberger with Geraldine Richelson, *Burnout: The High Cost of High Achievement* (New York, NY: Anchor Press, 1981).

Acknowledgments

Barna Group thanks the generous contributors whose voices and experiences enhanced the data and provided insight into the challenges and the promises of children's ministry today: Lacy Finn Borgo, Maureen Cooper, Cynthia Dixson, Dr. Denise Muir Kjesbo and Sam Luce.

The research team included Daniel Copeland, Savannah Kimberlin and Pam Jacob. Ashley Ekmay assisted with data verification. Alyce Youngblood produced the manuscript with support from Heather DalleTezze. Verónica Thames compiled Q&As. Doug Brown edited the manuscript. With creative direction from Joe Jensen, Chaz Russo designed the cover, and Rob Williams designed interior pages and data visualizations. Brenda Usery managed production. T'nea Rolle coordinated as project manager. Additional thanks for the support of our Barna colleagues: Jeni Cohen, Cicely Corry, Mel Grabendike, David Kinnaman, Dr. Charlotte Marshall Powell, Steve McBeth, Lauren Petersen, Matt Randerson, Layla Shahmohammadi, Chanté Smith and Todd White.

Finally, and importantly, Barna wishes to thank the team at Awana for their thoughtful partnership and their steadfast commitment to nurturing the faith of the next generation. They prepared a few words of gratitude of their own:

Proverbs 13:12 says, "Hope deferred makes the heart sick, but a longing fulfilled is a tree of life." You could say that this study, like that tree, is a bit life-giving to our team at Awana. It's a dream fulfilled and a prayer answered. For many of us in the Church who think critically and deeply about child faith formation, we've longed for a study like this. We've even grieved over the lack of "better metrics" within children's ministry. We believe that this study is the beginning of a new chapter within children's ministry. So, who do we have to thank for this?

Although the list is a bit long, it's just a small representation of the deep gratitude we feel for all who came together to make this dream a reality as we shape the future of the church together.

A hearty *thank you* to those who inspired our thinking: Jesus Christ our King, William F. Meehan III and Kim Starky Jonker in their work *Engine of Impact*, Jimmy Mellado of Compassion International, numerous friends in Christian higher education, the Children's Spirituality Summit, the Child Discipleship Forum community, our *RESILIENT* readership, the children's ministry leaders and pastors who dare to ask the hard questions, Katie Markins and various works by John Mark Comer, Mark Sayers, David Kinnaman, Mark Matlock, Gabe Lyons, Tony Evans, Kara Powell, Albert Mohler, Christian Smith, Francis Schaeffer, Darren Whitehead, Jon Tyson, Dallas Willard, George Barna, Dietrich Bonhoeffer, Pete Scazzero and Ed Stetzer.

A standing ovation to those who captured the vision and did the work: Mark McPeak, Mike Handler, Kevin White, Brian Rhodes, Ed Gossien, Valerie Bell, Steve Cohoon, Beth Bedoe, Kevin Orris, Chip Root, Sara Dudt, Ken Toeller, Kellie Bartley, Colin Robinson, Yeli Acevedo, Tom Chilton, Gajendra Tamang, Stephen Maphosah, Miguel Perez, Mark Campbell, Peter Mayberry, Dan Lovaglia, the Awana Board of Directors, the amazing team at Barna Group and Matt Markins.

And to our generous donors and ministry partners—you know who you are. You are true ministry partners. We are beyond grateful for you, and we love you deeply. What could be more important than forming children as resilient disciples of Jesus Christ? Let's go far together. ●

About the Project Partners

BARNA GROUP is a research firm dedicated to providing actionable insights on faith and culture, with a particular focus on the Christian Church. Since 1984, Barna has conducted more than two million interviews in the course of thousands of studies and has become a go-to source for organizations that want to better understand a complex and changing world from a faith perspective. Barna's clients and partners include a broad range of academic institutions, churches, nonprofits and businesses, such as Alpha, the Templeton Foundation, Fuller Seminary, the Bill and Melinda Gates Foundation, Maclellan Foundation, DreamWorks Animation, Focus Features, Habitat for Humanity, The Navigators, NBC-Universal, the ONE Campaign, Paramount Pictures, the Salvation Army, Walden Media, Sony and World Vision. The firm's studies are frequently quoted by major media outlets such as *The Economist*, BBC, CNN, *USA Today*, the *Wall Street Journal*, Fox News, *The Washington Post*, Huffington Post, *The New York Times* and the *Los Angeles Times*.
barna.com

AWANA is a global nonprofit organization, fueled by the generous donations of individuals, churches and organizations as well as resource sales to accomplish the mission of equipping leaders to reach kids with the gospel and engage them in lifelong discipleship. Awana's vision is that every child would come to know, love and serve the Lord Jesus Christ. Right now, this is happening in 130 countries worldwide through 63,000 churches reaching over 4.8 million kids with lasting faith. ●
awana.org

Knowledge to Lead with Confidence in Your Church and in Your Home

Guiding Children

This report studies Christian parents' deepest pain points, greatest concerns and dearest hopes for their children's faith formation—and their expectations for how their church can partner with them.

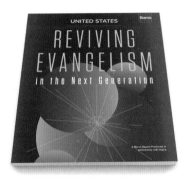

Reviving Evangelism in the Next Generation

The Church will be shaped by the attitudes and approaches young people bring to evangelism. Find out what the future may hold—and how you can guide and support our youth in making disciples.

Households of Faith

Learn how faith is being nurtured in homes—with the spouses, children, parents, roommates and even frequent visitors who spend time under our roofs—in a vivid portrait of the domestic lives of U.S. practicing Christians.

The Tech-Wise Family

The choices we make about technology can have consequences we may never have considered for our children and families. This book draws on Barna data to challenge and reimagine the way we use digital media.

AVAILABLE AT BARNA.COM/RESOURCES